SEEKING THE
BELOVED

A PRAYER JOURNEY WITH

ST. JOHN OF THE CROSS

SEEKING THE BELOVED

A PRAYER JOURNEY WITH

ST. JOHN OF THE CROSS

Wayne Simsic

Published by The Word Among Us Press
7115 Guilford Road
Frederick, Maryland 21704
wau.org

16 15 14 13 12   1 2 3 4 5
ISBN: 978-1-59325-201-4
eISBN: 978-1-59325-436-0

Unless otherwise noted, Scripture citations are from the New Jerusalem Bible, copyright © 1985 by Darton, Longman, & Todd, Ltd., and Doubleday, a division of Bantam Doubleday Dell Publishing Group, Inc. Reprinted by permission.

Scripture texts marked "NRSV" are taken from the New Revised Standard Version Bible: Catholic Edition, copyright © 1989, 1993, both by the Division of Christian Education of the National Council of the Churches of Christ in the USA. All rights reserved. Used with permission.

Quotations of St. John of the Cross taken from *The Collected Works of St. John of the Cross*, translated by Kieran Kavanaugh and Otilio Rodriguez, copyright © 1964, 1979, 1991 by Washington Province of Discalced Carmelites, ICS Publications, 2131 Lincoln Road, N.E. Washington, DC 20002-1199 USA, www.icspublications.org.
Reprinted by permission.

Cover design by Faceout Studio

Library of Congress Cataloging-in-Publication Data

Simsic, Wayne.
 Seeking the beloved : a prayer journey with St. John of the Cross / Wayne Simsic.
   p. cm.
 Includes bibliographical references (p.   ).
 ISBN 978-1-59325-201-4
 1. John of the Cross, Saint, 1542-1591. 2. Spiritual life—Catholic Church. 3. Prayer—Catholic Church. 4. Mysticism—Catholic Church. I. Title.
 BX4700.J7S56 2012
 248.3--dc23
                    2012002012

For Sr. Mercia Madigan, OSU,

and in memory of my mother,
Susan A. Simsic.

ACKNOWLEDGMENTS

This book was written while my mother was dying. Her spirit not only informs the text but also heightens my appreciation of John's uncompromising search for union with God. I carry her presence with me as I recall how enriching the writing of this book has been.

A unique group of men and women in my seminar on St. John of the Cross, offered through the Cleveland Ecumenical Institute for Religious Studies, journeyed with me together with the manuscript for six weeks. They shared their wisdom and nurtured a prayerful atmosphere throughout the six-week program. I am very grateful to these companions on the way.

Patricia Mitchell, my editor, has guided me through three books now at The Word Among Us Press. She has been a warm and encouraging source of support, for which I am deeply grateful.

Finally, this book reflects relationships with family and friends that have encouraged my efforts. However, I am, in particular, deeply grateful for my wife, Diana, whose love, support, and encouragement have been an ongoing source of strength and inspiration.

Table of Contents

Abbreviations Used in This Book

Ascent: *The Ascent of Mount Carmel*
Canticle: *The Spiritual Canticle*
Dark Night: *Dark Night*
Flame: *The Living Flame of Love*
Sayings: *Sayings of Light and Love*
Letters: *Letters*

Note: For those unfamiliar with John's writings, it is important to know that his major works are poems, which are followed by his own extensive commentary on each line and stanza. In this book, the poetry quoted will be followed by the stanza number, while the commentary will include the Roman numeral designating which book of the commentary is being cited (if applicable), as well as the chapter and paragraph number.

ST. JOHN OF THE CROSS
AS OUR GUIDE

Especially at a time of vulnerability, we often become aware of a hunger for a deeper relationship with God. We acknowledge that beneath the surface of our lives is an inner realm where a God of love breathes the gift of life into us moment to moment, calling us to intimacy. Yet we struggle to respond.

In particular, we find it difficult to pray consistently because distractions waylay our attention and the chaos and confusion of daily life throw us off course. We blame ourselves for not having the discipline or enough time. Though there may be some truth in this self-appraisal, perhaps a different approach to praying may shed some light on our difficulties.

What if our prayer struggle was due to a limited understanding of prayer? For example, we may think of prayer primarily as a method or technique or time set aside, rather than as an ongoing relationship with a loving God that will inevitably transform our lives. If prayer is a relationship with divine love, it is life itself. It is openness to the divine in all aspects of our everyday experience: the work we engage in, the conversations we have with a friend or our spouse, or the simple pleasure of a cup of coffee.

Certainly we need to set aside time for prayer each day to nurture our love for God, but the wider issue is our willingness to turn to God not only on particular occasions but as the center of our lives. This single-minded choice for God is prayer. It is an attitude or disposition of the heart that exists whether we are reflecting on Scripture or putting our children to bed. Just as any love relationship continues even if we are not thinking about or actually addressing the other person, our relationship with God continues whether we are engaged in formal prayer or not.

This may not make prayer easier, but it does take away the guilt and focuses our attention on love. Yet real love is never satisfied but seeks deeper and deeper expression. Our prayer, then, moves naturally toward greater intimacy with God, from a prayer that depends on the act of directing our minds and hearts to God to a level of simple intimacy and wordless communion. How does this journey unfold? This is where a spiritual guide like St. John of the Cross can help us.

What Is Prayer?

St. John of the Cross thought of prayer primarily as an intimate relationship with God. The important thing for John is not a particular method for praying but a relationship that moves toward communion with the divine. He believed that we are all meant for happiness with God. Each of us is unique in the way we progress, but nevertheless, each of us has the same ultimate goal.

If prayer is fundamentally an expression of love—a single-hearted reaching out to the Other in a love relationship—it is more simple than any technique or way of praying. The most important thing in prayer is the heart's inclination in relation to God.

Do I love God? Am I working to put my relationship with God at the center of my life? If I am, then this intention of heart will transform my day; I will want to live in the loving Presence at the center of my being and find ways to be attentive to it. Times of prayer will be times to nurture this presence more intimately and anchor myself in God, even when I feel that nothing is happening. It is like two people who love one another making time to be together—time to share the day and time to share a silence based on the mutual trust that has grown through the years.

It sounds simple, but we intellectualize relationships too quickly, even our relationship with God, and tend to put the cart before the horse. We find it easier to think about God rather than opening ourselves to the experience of the divine, to emphasize a way or method of prayer rather than taking an honest look at our present relationship with God. After all, relationships invite radical change and threaten the comfortable limits we place on love. Why open our heart to Someone more intimate to us than we are to ourselves? It is as if we choose to live with a spouse but never bother to address that person intimately.

For John of the Cross, authentic prayer is not a static experience but a journey that involves the whole self, physical and spiritual, in a dynamic process toward the realization of our divine and human destiny: union with God. It is an ascent that leads to inner transformation (*The Ascent of Mount Carmel*), a nighttime adventure to be united with the Beloved (*The Dark Night*), or a search brought on by the realization of the Beloved's absence (*The Spiritual Canticle*). Overall, it is a journey that passes from dusk, through midnight, toward dawn.

John addresses anyone, religious and layperson, who is serious about faith and therefore willing to respond without reserve to the grace of divine intimacy. In his eyes, we are each like the rich young man who keeps the commandments but must choose whether he is willing to give up everything for the sake of eternal life (Matthew 19:16-22).

Our Spiritual Guide

People today seem to be interested in prayer and turning inward more than ever before. We have experienced the turmoil and uncertainty of living in the secular culture of the modern world and realize the importance of cultivating a spiritual life. We have watched external structures, civil and religious, falter or crumble entirely, reminding us of how changeable the world can be. For many, a life transition or the death of a loved one has awakened them to a spiritual hunger they can no longer ignore.

There are also some people who hunger for a prayer deeper than words or thoughts about God. They know it is time to stop *talking* about divine love and *experience* it. They desire a union with God in a silent, wordless communion called "contemplation." Contemplative prayer is no longer seen as being reserved for the few but as a grace open to all who desire to live in the love of God. John would agree, emphasizing that we are meant to know God not from a distance but intimately. Jesus himself withdrew to the desert to nurture a profoundly intimate relationship with his Father.

Those who take seriously the move inward quickly recognize that they need guidance in listening to the Spirit, both during prayer and in ordinary life events. More aware of the Spirit's presence and energy, they need help discerning where they are being led on their faith journey. Going it alone and unguided is no longer an option.

I have to admit that when I first encountered John in my studies, I had a difficult time embracing him as a prayer guide. I had categorized him as a learned mystic, a saint, and a doctor of the church, and so I placed him on a pedestal far removed from my experience. This image, of course, does not fit St. Teresa of Ávila's comment about John: "I have not found in all Castile another like him, who can so inspire one with fervor on the path to heaven."[1]

Reading the writings of Thomas Merton was a breakthrough for me because I saw how much John of the Cross had influenced the young monk's spirituality and changed his life. Merton found in John a call to contemplative freedom beyond egoism, beyond spiritual ambition and methods of prayer, a call to be guided simply by God.[2] My growing familiarity with the spirituality of Teresa of Ávila, Thérèse of Lisieux, Brother Lawrence, Edith Stein, and other Carmelites also broadened my awareness of John of the Cross and his influence.

However, it was only when I began to direct retreats focused on the prayer and spirituality of John that my attitude changed dramatically. Like me, many of the retreatants had preconceived ideas about the mystic that prevented them from fully appreciating him. Some had locked horns with his writings on an intellectual level and missed the spirit of the text. One woman admitted that she had "hammered away" at the treatises to find meaning and in the process lost sight of the reason she was originally drawn to the saint: his total love for God and for people.

I approached the first retreats with some apprehension, assuming that we would spend most of the time clarifying the meaning of the texts. Before focusing on the treatises, however, I introduced images from John's poetry. Many responded enthusiastically because the images resonated with their own experience. These discussions opened the door to both John's spirit and his thought. Though he was highly educated in philosophy and theology, John was primarily a poet, and he knew the power of poetry, not simply as an art form, but as a primal expression of the inner life. In his own creative process, he wrote poems first, and only later, when pressed for an explanation, did he describe his meaning in prose commentaries.

I also focused on John's path of love. Many tend to emphasize the importance of faith in the journey through the dark night and forget that this journey begins with and is sustained by love. For John, the spiritual adventure involves both love and faith; love fires the heart and faith trusts that even in darkness, we are guided.

At the end of the retreats, I was surprised to see how many had responded to John in a personal way. Quite a few of the retreatants had been deeply moved by John's longing for God's love, and reading his words enkindled this ache in them. Others focused on his relentless search for union with God. A number of the retreatants realized that they had been practicing some form of silent prayer all along, aware of God's presence throughout the day and taking time to rest in it, but had not named the experience. Some indicated their intent to explore forms of contemplation such as centering prayer, and they wanted to know ways of integrating the contemplative experience into everyday life, liturgy, and the reading of Scripture.

Finally, the dark night was a subject that many identified with in their own faith journeys. Some examples of this "dark night" included a lack of fruitfulness in ministry, struggles with caregiving, difficulty in choosing a direction in life, problems with addictive behavior, personal crises, and the disorientation experienced in religious communities or the culture at large. They also found John's dark night to be an excellent antidote for the tendency today to sentimentalize religion or seek signs and visions rather than God himself.

An Overview

This book, then, builds on the inspiration I have received as a gift from these retreats, as well as on my study under the guidance of Carmelite scholars who have been a generous source of knowledge, and, of course, on John of the Cross himself, whose writings and presence have become an ongoing source of inspiration and guidance in my spiritual life.

The first chapter of *Seeking the Beloved* concentrates on John's insistence that we must first experience a longing for God before we can become serious about beginning a journey of love and faith. This longing in itself is the ongoing prayer of *The Spiritual Canticle*. Next, in chapter two, we explore *The Ascent of Mount Carmel* and *The Dark Night* as they relate to the redirection of desire toward God's love. Though this redirection of desire is not in itself prayer, it is essential for any growth in prayer.

Chapter three focuses on the importance of Christ as the axis for prayer and the spiritual journey, and this discussion leads to a description in chapter four of the transition from meditation or reflective prayer to contemplation, which is a silent, imageless prayer. Chapters five and six explore the dark night and what it means to trust in the life-giving power of this dark contemplation. I also invite participation from the reader with reflection questions at the end of each chapter.

This small book is neither a complete summary of John's spirituality of prayer nor an attempt to break new ground in discussing it. Rather, it introduces John as a wise and personal guide for our prayer lives and attempts to awaken and reinforce the voice of the Spirit in our hearts. John's wisdom directs us with authenticity and power, luring us into the deepest caverns of our hearts. We only need to say yes to this invitation.

A Brief Introduction to the Life of St. John of the Cross

It is easy to approach John with misconceptions about the kind of person he was and, as a result, write him off as an ascetic whose spirituality has little to do with us. We may think that he focused on an otherworldly dimension far removed from the earthly reality that we engage in day to day. Nothing could be further from the truth—even a passing familiarity with the events of his life reveals a different picture. He was a poet and artist as well as a wise and down-to-earth administrator who did not shy away from manual labor. He loved creation, tended gardens, was profoundly influenced by women, and taught the importance of both body and soul for spiritual growth. When he died, large numbers of the poor visited his body, and he was revered by common people as a holy man.

John lived in sixteenth-century Spain. Some of the conditions existing at that time would be difficult to imagine today: a wide chasm between the nobility and the poor; the lifestyle of the poor (including John's widowed mother, who traveled from city to city searching for means to survive); deaths from malnutrition (including John's brother Luis); the loss of life from plagues and epidemics; and the dangers of life on the road (swollen streams, bandits, primitive way stations) that often forced a traveler to write a will before journeying. Ironically, all of this was occurring at a time when Spain was being nourished by creative energy and achievements in politics, culture, and religion. In fact, the time period would eventually be referred to historically as the "Golden Age."

John of the Cross was born Juan de Yepes y Álvarez in 1542 in Fontiveros, Spain, on the feast day of St. John the Baptist. John's father, Gonzalo de Yepes, came from a family of rich silk merchants, but he fell into disfavor when, for love alone, he married Catalina Álvarez, a poor weaver beneath his social class. This love, born out of the extraordinary sacrifice of an inheritance and a prestigious family name, became a guiding star for John throughout his life. Later, as he fell in love with God, he recognized that all should be left behind in pursuit of love alone.

Not only were John and his two older brothers, Francisco and Luis, born into poverty, but when John was still a child, his father died from a widespread contagion that spread throughout

Spain. A year later, Luis also died, probably from malnutrition. Poverty pressed down relentlessly on the mother and her two children. When she turned to her husband's family for help, they rejected her outright.

It is easy to understand how suffering came to play a major role in John's life. The family moved to Medina del Campo, where Catalina and her sons attempted to earn a living as weavers. They lived a hand-to-mouth existence. Nevertheless, Catalina not only found time and energy to take care of her sons but helped needy people, such as an orphan she found in the street one day. Both John and Francisco were deeply influenced by their mother's example, and though less well-known than his brother, Francisco would undergo a conversion and dedicate his life to the sick and poor.

John had a strong sense of the feminine, cultivated not only by his relationship with his mother but later by Teresa of Ávila, as well as the women, lay and religious, under his spiritual direction. Another feminine influence became apparent at school one day when John, while playing with schoolmates in a courtyard, fell into a deep well. It must have been a dramatic incident because his friends thought he had drowned. However, John floated to the top, was pulled out, and maintained that he had been miraculously saved by the Blessed Mother. For the rest of his life, he sought out Mary for guidance, and many assume that it was his Marian devotion that led him to the Carmelites.

It is interesting to note that as a young boy attending a vocational school for orphans and the poor, John not only had a roof over his head and learned how to read and write, but he also learned the rudiments of carpentry, tailoring, wood carving, and painting. This practical education served him well for the rest of his life, and images from the trades and the arts are sprinkled throughout his writings. We envision him as a spiritual master, but he also helped construct aqueducts and monasteries, often hauling stone and laying brick. He enjoyed hands-on activities like gardening, and in his free time, he could be found pulling weeds and harvesting vegetables.

As an adolescent, John lived at a hospital, the Hospital of the Conception, which was devoted to victims of the plague and those dying from contagious diseases. No doubt the images of disease and suffering that he witnessed firsthand there stayed with him for the rest of his life. John could often be found inside comforting the dying or outside on the streets, soliciting funds for the hospital. Later, as a Carmelite prior, he tended the sick under his care and went out of his way to help those who were poorer than he was. The administrator of the hospital recognized the young man's extraordinary compassion and dedication and wanted John to be ordained and serve as hospital chaplain. But in a decision that would change his life forever, John chose to enter the Carmelite Order, where he could follow his growing love for prayer and solitude.

After joining the Carmelites, John pursued studies at the University of Salamanca, one of the finest European universities at the time. He distinguished himself in his studies and cultivated a disciplined mind, but his main interest was not in academics but in spiritual development. At the time he followed—too enthusiastically—a spiritual discipline that involved prayer, fasting, and various forms of asceticism. Later, however, he recognized that excessive asceticism was self-serving, and he directed people toward a more balanced spirituality.

He met Teresa of Ávila about the time he celebrated his first Mass as a newly ordained priest. Teresa was looking for someone to assist with a reform movement. She was interested in returning to the original rule of the order—regular community life, fasting, silence, poverty, and prayer. These reform communities would be referred to as "Discalced," which means "without shoes," a characteristic common to religious communities at the time who identified with the poor. Though Teresa was twenty-seven years older than John, the two became fast friends, sharing wisdom and affection. John considered Teresa his mentor, and she recognized him as a spiritual equal. They exchanged poetry and missed each other's presence when separated for too long of a time.

Under Teresa's guidance, John and two other friars began a reformed community in a small ramshackle house at Duruelo, not far from Ávila. John changed his name to "John of the Cross," and his mother, brother, and sister-in-law joined him. The primitive conditions, the hard manual labor, his apostolic outreach to a neighboring village, and the peaceful rural surroundings were perfect for his prayer life, and John thrived. It is important to note that even with his deep love of solitude, he did not isolate himself, but included his family, friars, and the surrounding community in his spiritual experience.

The community thrived, and some time later, at Teresa's request, John was assigned to be confessor and spiritual director at the Convent of the Incarnation in Ávila, where Teresa had been appointed prioress by the ecclesiastical superior. For the next five years, John lived in a hut at the edge of the property. He said Mass, heard confessions, taught catechism to local children, and gave spiritual direction to both nuns and laypeople. His gift for spiritual direction developed significantly as he learned subtle ways to influence the inner growth of those under his guidance. He helped Teresa herself to enter deeper into her prayer life.

An important turning point in John's spiritual life came with his imprisonment in Toledo. The reform that was originally supported by some leaders in the Carmelite Order became a source of division and anger. John stayed out of the wrangling but still became the focus of attention due to his role as founding member. A meeting of the Carmelites condemned the reform movement, and John—unsuspecting—was arrested on December 2, 1577, and led off to Toledo. The Carmelites who were not part of Teresa's reform movement took him to their monastery and threw him into a small cell that had once served as a latrine. He was flogged, starved, and told to forsake his commitment to the primitive rule. These nine months of suffering became John's "dark night."

It would be tempting to concentrate on the betrayal and suffering, but the seemingly endless days of imprisonment became for John a time of praying the breviary and writing down in a notebook devotional pieces and poems. The darkness and isolation did not bring him to despair but became the environment in which he nourished his relationship with his Beloved. It inspired a song that took the form of his poetic masterpieces *The Dark Night of the Soul* and *The Spiritual Canticle*. Clearly, the stark emptiness of the prison experience was no sterile environment but a fertile ground for prayer and creativity.

One night, through his own watchfulness and planning,

John escaped and hid with Discalced nuns in their monastery in Toledo. Even though his enemies kept guard on the monastery, the nuns kept him away from his captors and saw that John received medical help.

Meanwhile, after a long and complicated process, the Discalced became a separate province in 1581 and were allowed to govern themselves. John was named superior of their monastery at El Calvario. He gladly retreated to this place of natural beauty, where he could often be found completely absorbed in God while gazing at the landscape. He urged his friars to relax in the woods and countryside, and he found a place to pray on the side of a mountain where the view was spectacular. When priors from other monasteries visited John unexpectedly, they would often find him working in the garden, his hands caked with dirt.

John eventually found himself at a monastery in Granada. He remained there for six years, which were perhaps the most fruitful years of his life. He worked on a design for the monastery, undertook the construction of an aqueduct to water the gardens so that food could be grown for the friars and the poor, and built a cloister. Both he and his brother, Francisco, made the bricks and laid them. Besides his duties as prior, he was a spiritual director for a community of reformed Carmelite nuns, and their questions about prayer and the spiritual life inspired his writing. Generally, his writings were not meant for academics but were a response to the spiritual needs of nuns, friars, novices, and laywomen. They were inspirational, not intellectual exercises.

At Granada he completed *The Spiritual Canticle*, wrote the *The Living Flame of Love*, and finished *The Ascent of Mount*

Carmel and *The Dark Night*. In time he was elected vicar provincial; traveling frequently, he founded seven monasteries and gave spiritual direction. While visiting communities, he continued to help out, building stone walls, making bricks, and tending vegetable gardens.

In 1588 John became prior in Segovia and was elected a councilor to the vicar general, Nicolas Doria. Because he differed with the domineering vicar general, John fell out of favor and was sent to an isolated monastery as punishment, although he enjoyed the solitude and opportunity to pray. However, two friars began building a case against him in an attempt to have him dismissed from the Discalced community. This process stopped when John became ill from a fever caused by a serious inflammation in his leg.

Surgery on his leg proved fruitless; nothing could stop the spread of gangrene. Realizing that he was about to die, John listened to a reading from the Song of Songs and began to prepare himself. According to one of his biographers, shortly after midnight when the bell rang for Matins, he asked,

> "What was that?" "The bell calling the brothers to Matins," they answered. "Glory to God. I shall say them in heaven," he replied, looking at each one as if giving them a personal message.[3]

Moments later on the fourteenth day of December 1591, John of the Cross, builder, leader, spiritual director, writer, poet, and mystic, died. He was forty-nine years old.

John's Voice Today

John awakens us to our potential in God at a time when the world suffers from a lack of hope. We hear the news of the world today and recognize the need for healing, for a sense of hope that goes beneath the daily images of war and disaster. We ache for a deeper perspective on our personal lives and on the world at large.

Where do we begin? Following John of the Cross and other mystics, we need to cultivate a contemplative disposition, to learn to listen to the subtle whisper of the Spirit in our daily lives. A deeper listening opens us to the presence of God in Scripture and in ordinary events. It gives us the strength to be a prophetic witness in difficult times.

In other words, we have to grow in prayer. How many have felt the call to deeper prayer but ignored it because it did not fit into their preconceived image of the spiritual life or because they could not envision how to integrate a deeper communion with God into their lives? John's example suggests that it is not the intricacy of contemplation that keeps us at a distance but the simplicity. Contemplation is too innocent, too childlike, and too immediate to be entertained by our sophisticated world view. To put it another way, how many are called to rest in the depths of silence but settle for the turmoil of a life lived on the surface? John of the Cross insists that the grace of contemplative prayer—a grace meant for all—cannot be ignored without peril.

As John shows us, this path of contemplation does not enlarge the ego but is a path of humility—the humility of the cross—which leads to the light of the resurrection. It is not a path of cultural approval because it smashes false gods and destroys the idols upon which we have come to depend. We have a choice: to seek ultimate love and purity of heart or settle for a life limited by a false reality. For John, it all comes down to our desire to live as a disciple of Jesus Christ and to work with the Spirit to establish the kingdom of God on earth.

Finally, John reminds us of a truth that we easily forget and find difficult to accept: It is all about love. In the words of theologian Leonard Doohan, "God draws people to divine life, taking the initiative in every stage of the journey. God's love precedes all human response; it is love that calls, purifies, illumines, supports in pain, shares, transforms, and unites."[4]

CHAPTER ONE

LONGING FOR LOVE

How gently and lovingly
you wake in my heart,
where in secret you dwell alone.
—*The Living Flame of Love*, stanza 4

A heartfelt yearning for the divine opens John of the Cross' poem *The Spiritual Canticle* and invites us on a journey of love that usurps all other concerns:

Where have you hidden,
Beloved, and left me moaning? (stanza 1)

For John, love of God is the reason we exist; it is our heart's deepest passion: "The ultimate reason for everything is love" (*Canticle* 38.5). To read his poem is to recognize that the primary purpose of our life and our prayer is to uncover a love relationship with God. John's laser-like focus on union with the divine challenges us to a rediscovery of self and a commitment to a journey of faith and love.

What is prayer but falling in love with God? This may be difficult to admit because it makes us vulnerable and challenges us to let go of the brackets we put around divine intimacy. We accept prayer as a relationship but usually define the relationship according to our own limitations; after all, we are fearful not knowing where this love will lead. John invites intimacy beyond anything we could imagine, a complete dedication to the Source of love. This message resonates throughout his prose commentary but especially in his poetry.

When does the spiritual adventure begin? It begins when we discover divine intimacy as the very ground of our being, at the center of who we are. John reminds us that each person is meant for God; each of us has the capacity for transcendence, for union with the divine. God lives in the depths of our being, imparting to us life, dignity, and love: "You yourself are his dwelling" (*Canticle* 1.7). It is easy to assume that union with God is a concern limited to saints and mystics, that it involves special gifts beyond the ordinary. John, however, extends the invitation to everyone, asking us to respond according to our unique experience. However, this is the critical issue: What is my heart's inclination? Does it lean toward a multitude of concerns or toward one primary concern—God?

Some may be put off by John's stark language and his emphasis on radical surrender. His teaching may seem overwhelming, but his words should be translated only in the context of a love relationship. When there is a choice made for love, then renunciation follows naturally. John seemed to emphasize this point with a group of nuns who found his *Ascent of Mount Carmel* harsh; he referred them to his poetry, suggesting that they should begin with the experience that had inspired him.

John emphasizes that the power of our love to influence God should not be taken lightly. As he puts it, "The power and tenacity of love is great, for love captures and binds God himself" (*Canticle* 32.1). How amazing it is to think that whether we are conscious of it or not, we have the capacity to hold God close through love. Prayer does more than get God's attention—it forges the bonds of relationship. Rest assured, John tells us, that a loving heart knows God intimately.

Seek God by Day

Those who seek God and yet want to find their own satisfaction and rest seek him at night and thus will not find him. Those who look for him through the practices and works of virtues and get up from the bed of their own satisfaction and delight seek him by day and thus will find him. (Canticle 3.3)

It is difficult to think of God as the primary love of our lives, as John invites, because we do not know what we really want. We lack the single-heartedness, or in a term familiar to spiritual adventurers through the ages, "purity of heart."

We are pulled in a number of directions by a multitude of desires. We desire God, but God is only one concern among many. As John puts it, we seek God at night without much interest rather than by day with wholehearted effort. We need to make a choice to seek God by day. John haunts us with this question: What is your ultimate desire, what will make you completely happy? If we truly want God, we will have God; if we seek something else, then that is where our heart is.

Insights of this importance cannot remain as inspirational thoughts; they need to be integrated into our lives. If we truly desire God, then divine love has to be at the center of our everyday experience, at the center of the person that we are in all of our activity. We have to wake up each day with the thought of divine nearness and with a prayer of gratitude. Why such a complete dedication? Because God is the source of our existence; there is no way to compartmentalize Mystery—it is our life.

The fullness of this insight may not come easily, but when it does, it is life transforming. Referring to his own sudden awareness of being completely dependent on God's presence moment to moment, theologian William Shannon writes, "I could see that all the joys I had in life, however great or small they might be, existed only because of this most radical joy that came from the fact that I have been blessed with the grace of existence—a grace that could not *be* apart from the presence of God."[5]

We do not claim God as our ultimate desire, says John, because of the cost involved (*Canticle* 3.2). We want the security and comfort of our present lives; we do not want to sacrifice more than what is convenient, and even if we experience love in our lives, we still allow ourselves to be mired in useless desires and a false sense of security. It is as if we were asleep and know that we need to wake up, rise from our bed, and face the daylight, but instead, we choose to slump back into the seductive warmth of our old ways. In the end, we choose illusion over reality.

Even the thought of handing over our lives strikes fear in our hearts. Would not such a complete surrender lessen our appreciation of the world around us? In fact, as John teaches, being God-centered does not diminish enjoyment of life but allows us to appreciate it as gift and, paradoxically, to embrace it with even greater intensity because we no longer take it for granted. It is not the pleasure seeker who passionately enjoys creation but the one who acknowledges its source. John did not war against the senses but refused to let something less than God take the place of divine love.

This is John's primary message: Our suffering will continue unless we seek union with God because anything less than infinite love will never satisfy our heart's desire. Creation is good and beautiful but it is limited. John knew suffering throughout his life—poverty, hunger, abandonment—and recognized that the most profound suffering occurs in a heart separated from God. Henri Nouwen once confessed, "Coming home and staying there where God dwells, listening to the voice of truth and love, that was indeed, the journey I most feared because I knew that God was a jealous lover who wanted every part of me all the time."[6]

So how do we seek God by day? John suggests prayer, a practice of the virtues of faith, hope, and love, and control of our harmful desires. Go to your room and pray to God in secret and discipline your pleasure-seeking inclinations. Through prayer, we gain self-knowledge, and through control of harmful desires, we are able to seek God without being waylaid by needless detours. Prayer and sacrifice—these are the two traditional spiritual disciplines that allow the yearning for God that has been buried under distractions and busyness to rise up in our consciousness and prevent us from falling asleep. John warns that not any prayer will do: "Many desire that God cost them no more than words, and even these they say badly" (*Canticle* 3.2). Prayer involves the whole self. We need to rise from our bed and begin a serious search for God through the day, not concerned with the sacrifice this entails.

Begin with Experience

If anyone is seeking God, the Beloved is seeking that person much more. (Flame 3.28)

A woman on a retreat I was directing approached me with some hesitation and said she had recently felt an overwhelming presence of God during prayer. She experienced God as a warmth that rose up from the depths of her being, assuring her that she was loved unconditionally. As she talked, her hands stretched outward as if to express the expansiveness of the experience; her voice filled with wonder and awe, and her eyes welled up with tears. I listened, at a loss for words. Later at a lunch break, she pulled me aside to apologize for what she called an "emotional display," but in the same breath, she whispered, "It's all true."

John insists that our spirituality be rooted in our experience of being loved by God. We find it easy to share most of our life experiences, but sadly, we often become reticent when sharing the experience of divine love. The grace-filled experience this woman described often accompanies growth in prayer, and it has roots in ancient Christian tradition. A warm sensation swells the heart at an unexpected time and flows through the person. Spiritual guides like John caution that the experience is a gift, and though we can prepare ourselves to receive it, it should not be sought after. If we listen to the faith stories that people share, we learn that each of us, in our own time, can experience what John calls "a living flame of love" and what the author of the fourteenth-century spiritual classic *The Cloud of Unknowing* refers to as a "blind stirring of love." It can address us with drama, like the visions of Jeremiah or Isaiah, or the flash of light that blinded Paul on the road to Damascus. Or it can call us quietly, like the still small voice that spoke to Elijah, and it can repeat itself in our hearts throughout the years.

It is important to appreciate what slow learners we are when it comes to love. We may not be able to describe God's influence on our hearts, but we can learn to trust it and respond. God loved us first: "Let us love, then, because he first loved us" (1 John 4:19). How can we not respond? The first lines of *The Spiritual Canticle* that opened this chapter begin the story of a person in search of union with God. That journey is possible only if the person has first experienced God's love.

Faith tells us that God is within us, inviting us to a life of love no matter who we are or where we are on the road of life. Why not appreciate that we "are his dwelling and his secret inner room and hiding place. . . . What else do you search for outside, when within yourself you possess your riches, . . . your Beloved whom you desire and seek?" (*Canticle* 1.7, 8)? Why become anxious or fearful thinking that we have to find ways to bring God into our lives? The divine is already present, addressing us. Fear and anxiousness are the responses of a person who does not trust fully the love within him.

The secret source for the energy and fire of the prophets is not so much that they loved as their conviction of being loved without any merit on their part. They understood that from the beginning, they were touched by God: "Before I formed you in the womb I knew you" (Jeremiah 1:5). God's love is our first love. If we would allow ourselves to feel the awe of this intimacy, we could never remain the same. We would live each moment differently. We would begin to see through the eyes of this love and uncover, as John did, a mysterious light, not only in ourselves, but in others and creation. A leaf, an apple, a ray of sunlight, a stranger, a child—all become manifestations of a divine Artist.

John himself found the face of God in all creation because he was first able to discover the divine as the mirror of his own being. He saw all created reality as bursting with beauty. He could be found praying in the middle of the forest with arms outstretched or looking out a window transfixed by the view of the countryside. When he was at a monastery not far from Segovia, he found a place for solitude, a natural cave that overlooked a magnificent valley filled with vibrant color in the sparkling light. It was there that he would retreat to pray, allowing himself to be absorbed in a vision of beauty. Is it any wonder, then, that a verse like the following from *The Spiritual Canticle* should pour forth from his heart?

> O woods and thickets,
> planted by the hand of my Beloved!
> O green meadow,
> coated, bright, with flowers.
> tell me, has he passed by you? (stanza 4)

This experience of God's love—the "wound" of love, as John calls it—may reveal itself through creation and in prayer, but it may also come unexpectedly and more subtly through other life experiences, such as a love relationship with a spouse, the gift of friendship, or a severe illness. Or it may appear at a time in our lives when we feel pulled inward by an urgent whisper and discover the truth that we have been ignoring all along. In each case, we wake up to the presence of an inner wellspring that flows to the surface of our consciousness and breaks through, exposing us to the reality of a loving Presence. Knowing that we live in the mystery of this Presence, how can we not feel driven to uncover the holy in all aspects of our lives—in the day-to-day routine and in relationships, interests, activities, and the natural world?

It is important, then, to be attentive to the experiences of our lives as being layered with hidden meaning, circled around a core like the growth rings of a tree. As the nearness of the divine becomes more apparent, we take responsibility for this increased awareness and learn to listen more consistently and attentively to all aspects of our life story. Listening with faith, we remain in touch with a hidden center beneath thoughts and feelings, a center that will anchor us in any spiritual storm or inner upheaval.

To this end, any number of questions might be helpful. For example, when did I discover that my life held a deeper meaning, and how did I respond? When did I experience my life being hollowed out by suffering? Did this experience give me the capacity for greater joy? Do I recognize that the flame of love has been present all the time, waiting to draw me toward God?

Questions like these open the door to self-reflection; they also introduce us to a prayer that connects us to Life itself. Too often we segregate prayer from daily, mundane events, when these are the fertile ground for divine revelation.

Self-reflection also increases self-knowledge. We begin to see ourselves as we really are in the eyes of God—as a person with inherent self-worth. True self-knowledge is to realize that you are God's beloved child: "Before I formed you in the womb I knew you" (Jeremiah 1:5). This sense of self-worth is essential for the journey; without it we cannot become the person God wants us to be.

The Breath of Life

For the property of love is to make the lover equal to the object loved. . . . In this equality of friendship the possessions of both are held in common. (Canticle 28.1)

Recently I saw an elderly man walking in the park, pulling a canister of oxygen behind him. His slow gait, his bowed head, and the tank erratically weaving behind him held my attention. I thought of how essential breath is for life and how grateful I am for my own ability to breathe. Whenever I forget this lesson, I don't have long to wait before an onset of my own asthma reminds me of it.

As our lives unfold, love continues to pursue us, drawing us steadily closer to union with the Spirit of love, the breath of life. In *The Spiritual Canticle*, the soul turns to God and says, "Breathe through my garden," invoking a movement of love in the soul (stanza 17). On our part, we "breathe" God, but we may remain unaware that this breath feeds us, body and soul. According to John, the Spirit of love seeks to raise the soul to its level, to make the soul equal so that it can share all that it has. We may catch hints of our transformation from the human to the divine in this life, but the fullness of this state will be known only in eternal life.

How intimate is our relationship with God? John reminds us that we were created in the image of God, that we have divine life within us. This divine spark or seed of God holds within it all that we need to become like God. Our life journey is a process of assimilating the divine, opening ourselves more and more to its reality, and recognizing that we are already children of God. This gradual awakening takes place in the thicket of daily experience, through mundane events and everyday relationships both difficult and rewarding. All of these, in their own unique way, call us to be true to our inheritance. According to John, we are called to divinization because we are "truly gods by participation, equals and companions of God" (*Canticle* 39.6).

We may balk at the fullness of this participation; union with the divine seems incomprehensible given the limitations of the human spirit. John foresees our concern and replies, "One should not think it impossible that the soul be capable of so sublime an activity as this breathing in God, through participation as God breathes in her. . . . He created her in his image and likeness that she might attain such resemblance" (*Canticle* 39.4). It is so simple: We were created for union with God. We need to learn how to breathe, to open ourselves to the Spirit of love.

The Meaning of Love

It is the property of perfect love to be unwilling to take anything for self, nor does it attribute anything to self, but all to the beloved. (Canticle 32.2)

Talk of love in our culture can be confusing because it tends to focus primarily on an emotional state or a greeting-card sentiment. In mature relationships, emotions play a role, but they are not always present. Rather than being a passing feeling leaving us euphoric, mature love invites change—moving beyond the ego and giving ourselves for the sake of another. As John counseled, "Love consists not in feeling great things but in having great detachment and in suffering for the Beloved" (*Sayings* 115). He believed that love is a process of self-emptying for the sake of another.

We forget that love is not about what I can get but about what I can give. When we think of sacrifice for the sake of love, our thoughts tend to drift toward the possibility of getting something in return. The reason is that we assume the sacrifice will involve personal deprivation, so we look for a return on our good deeds. Applying this to our spiritual lives, we expect a good feeling from prayer, from attendance at liturgy, or from our sacrifices. In short, we are willing to give only for the sake of receiving.

John, however, thought of giving from another perspective. To love is to give but to give without a sense of being deprived. A lover simply gives from the heart, which is an infinite source of love; this is a sheer gift of self. Nothing is lost or taken away because this love has no limits. Also, this act of love, though a sacrifice of self, does not leave the lover in distress, worried about compensation, but rather becomes a state of joy. A lover who shares herself is sharing the life of the Spirit, and this selfless act overflows in buoyant goodwill.

When John was a prisoner, trapped in a small dark cell with a small beam of light overhead, you would think that reaching out to his jailer would have been the last thing on his mind. However, he consistently expressed gratitude, thanking the jailer for each small favor, and just before his escape, he offered him a gift of one of the two treasured items he possessed, a crucifix. He acted not from a sense of being deprived, though this could be justified by his suffering, but from a profound inner peace and loving generosity. Referring to a painful experience at the end of his life, he writes in a letter, "Think nothing else but that God ordains all, and where there is no love, put love, and you will draw out love" (*Letters* 26). He teaches us that abandonment to love, though difficult as it may be, does not lead to anxiousness and a sense of loss but to the freedom and joy of divine love.

For John, the story of love was never self-oriented. He watched his father sacrifice social prestige and wealth in order to marry his mother, a poor widow without social distinction. From this example and his humble origins, John knew that authentic love could demand tremendous sacrifice and that a love relationship with God would mean ongoing transformation. The flame of love never ceases to purify the heart in order that it can be free for the love of self, creation, and God. To make this point, John used the image of sunlight shining through a dirty window.

By wiping away the film, namely, all that is not God, we make a way for divine love to shine in the soul, and "the soul will be illumined by and transformed in God" (*Ascent* II.5.7).

It is significant, however, to recognize that this love will not allow us to make our lives partially available. It demands total presence: God wants the whole person. We may be hoping secretly to parcel out pieces of our lives to God and continue to shape our own version of self. John reminds us that the invitation of love invites something radical; it addresses us personally and with urgency. What can we do but implore the Spirit of Christ to guide us and give us strength and, to the best of our ability, open our hearts to receive the sun's rays?

The Spiritual Canticle

I went out calling you, but you were gone. (Canticle, stanza 1)

What better description of our journey toward loving union with God than the one found in the Song of Songs of the Old Testament? The soul, touched by love, hungers for more and is willing to risk an adventure of the unknown to find fulfillment: "Draw me in your footsteps, let us run" (Song of Songs 1:4). God, in turn, assures the soul that she is loved and prepared to respond to the call: "You are wholly beautiful, my beloved, and without blemish" (4:7).

John was so captivated by this passionate adventure that he memorized it and had the Song of Songs recited on his deathbed. He also created his own version, *The Spiritual Canticle*, during his imprisonment. The darkness and deprivation he experienced allowed him to explore the unconscious and to spontaneously respond to images that represented his own journey, in much the same way that Francis of Assisi composed his poem "The Canticle of Brother Sun" in the time leading up to his death. In both cases, a poem celebrating love and deeply sensitive to the beauty of creation arose from fertile darkness and profound faith. In both cases, an ongoing prayer of the heart, forged in the daily trials and joys for years, took flight and became a mystical song.

John recognized that poetic images more fully and spontaneously express the mystery of the heart's yearning for God than any prose rendition:

> Who can describe the understanding he gives to loving souls in whom he dwells? And who can express the experience he imparts to them? Who, finally, can explain the desires he gives them? Certainly, no one can! . . . As a result these persons let something of their experiences overflow in figures, comparisons, and similitudes, and from the abundance of their spirit pour out secrets and mysteries rather than rational explanations. (*Sayings*, Prologue)

This is clear acknowledgment that poetry is first-order language, and prose, second. John, for example, had a deep appreciation for the sensuous imagery of the Song of Songs. In *The Spiritual Canticle*, he conveys the passion and intimacy of God's personal love for us with a simple image like this one: "You considered / that one hair fluttering at my neck / . . . and it captivated you" (stanza 31).

We may be tempted to read John's poem from a safe personal distance, not quite sure whether we can really identify with the words. When we hear the cry, "Where have you hidden, / Beloved, and left me moaning?" (stanza 1), and accompany the searcher following the signs of the Beloved through creation, "O woods and thickets / . . . O green meadow / . . . tell me, has he passed by you?" (stanza 4), we wonder if on some level, we are experiencing the same ache. In particular, when the journey eventually leads the soul to the joy of union in "the sweet garden of her desire, / and she rests in delight, / laying her neck / on the gentle arms of her Beloved" (stanza 22) and becomes truly like God, we question whether this adventure can include us or is reserved for the few with special grace. John insists that the call is meant for every Christian, since each of us is called to divine union from the time of baptism; and the passionate relationship depicted in the *Canticle*, though integrated uniquely into each person's path toward union with God, should be ours.

The images surrounding the lover's pursuit of the Beloved invite us to explore the poetry of our own adventure and discover the aspects of a love relationship that speak to the longing of our own soul. Theologian John Welch suggests that the best way to read John is through a dialogue with our own lives and with an openness to the metaphors and symbols that have arisen in our own story. Discovering our own poetry, we find an entrance into the universal symbols of John's poems and let "story speak to story."[7]

FAITH AND LOVE: THE BLIND PERSON'S GUIDES

Seek him in faith and love, without desiring to find satisfaction in anything . . . other than what you ought to know. Faith and love are like the blind person's guides. They will lead you along a path unknown to you, to the place where God is hidden. (Canticle 1.11)

John joins this path of love described in the *Canticle* with the path of faith. The virtue of faith is a response to the call of grace; it is an invitation, an inner urging, and a feeling of being pulled toward a greater reality. Repeating the words of a character from one of Fyodor Dostoevsky's books, Dorothy Day wrote, "All my life I have been haunted by God."[8] This "haunting" is grace, a gift freely given by God (Ephesians 2:8). The choice to respond is always ours.

The path of faith is not a search for a conceptual knowledge about God, even though this can be attractive. It is not arrived at only through intelligence or by willing it to happen. We would not even desire to come to God unless God had already given us this hunger as a gift. However, an experience of a loving, caring, forgiving God at the heart of our daily lives—perhaps through the birth of a child or a tragic loss—can invite a faith response.

John teaches that faith leads into darkness, into a release of all the limited images and ideas of the divine, because God surpasses all these and cannot be limited. God is never simply "out there," but is both near and distant. We are limited to human intelligence; God is mystery. Though images may help in our growing friendship with the divine, they become a hindrance if we remain attached to them. Ultimately, God remains hidden, dwelling behind a cloud of unknowing. However, for John, God is not some abstraction or endless void, but a Trinitarian God who pours out the Word into creation and into history for all eternity.

We are called, then, to pass beyond our natural limits of understanding and imagination and enter into Mystery. The life of faith is a dark night—dark because our intellect cannot cope with the sheer luminosity of divine presence. Faith, however, steadily draws us into the darkness because it believes without seeing.

Interestingly, for John, darkness does not occur only at a certain point in our relationship with God but is ongoing throughout the spiritual journey. Faith constantly calls us beyond our limitations because we never really know God, so the darkness increases as our faith deepens. Often a crisis like the death of a parent or an unexpected illness introduces us to the darkness because it challenges our beliefs, and we are forced to reexamine our limited image of God and decide whether we will trust a mysterious, inviting, but challenging love.

It is difficult to accept and remember our human limitations when it comes to our experience and knowledge of God. Images of God become so comforting and consoling that we come to think that we truly know God, and this supposition leads us to take God for granted. We presume that we can carry God in our back pocket and call on the divine whenever necessary. However, in time we discover that the divine cannot be compartmentalized. God eludes us, and only "faith . . . gives and communicates God himself to us" (*Canticle* 12.4).

Love joins faith in showing us the way through the inevitable darkness that comes with spiritual growth. It is faith that prepares us for union with God by drawing us into the unknown, and it is love—the heart's longing for the divine—that provides light even in the thickest darkness of night. The author of Hebrews asks us to believe in "things not seen" or things that cannot be proved (11:1, NRSV). We may still cry out with the psalmist, "How long, Yahweh, will you forget me?" (Psalm 13:1), but with faith we believe that God does care and will answer our prayer and that God is looking after us and the cosmos. We can set our hearts on a God whose heart is set on us.

The path of loving faith leads to the summit of Mount Carmel, a climb into the deepening night where, as John reminds us, "The greater one's faith the closer is one's union with God" (*Ascent* II.9.1). Let us now turn our attention to this climb, which calls forth from us a deeper unity than we could ever imagine.

SUGGESTIONS FOR REFLECTION

1. Was your awakening to God's love gradual or sudden? Was it the result of a particular event or crisis in your life?

2. Describe one time when you experienced God's unconditional love and your own lovableness. Did this experience alter your life? How?

3. Read this passage from the Gospel of Luke:

> And now a lawyer stood up and, to test [Jesus], asked, "Master, what must I do to inherit eternal life?" He said to him, "What is written in the Law?

What is your reading of it?" He replied, "You must love the Lord your God with all your heart, with all your soul, with all your strength, and with all your mind, and your neighbor as yourself." Jesus said to him, "You have answered right, do this and life is yours." (Luke 10:25-28)

Invitations to give yourself completely to God's love come throughout the day. Take time to recall and reflect on the small invitations of love that you have experienced in the last few days.

4. John wrote, "Love is the soul's inclination, strength, and power for the soul in making its way to God, for love unites it with God. The more degrees of love it has, the more deeply it enters into God and centers itself in him" (*Flame* 1.13). Where in your life is God's love most evident? What do you think the Holy Spirit is asking of you?

CHAPTER TWO

THE REDIRECTION OF OUR DESIRES

When the will directs these faculties, passions,
and strivings to God, turning them away from all that is
not God, the soul preserves its strength for God, and comes
to love him with all its might.
—*The Ascent of Mount Carmel*, III.16.2

While walking in the woods in late summer one year, I came across a clearing and found blackberries ripening in the afternoon sun. The berries sparkled like small dark orbs. After tasting the sweetness of the first one, I eagerly gathered the closest berries and eventually extended my arm further into the thicket to pluck the ones just out of reach. In no time small thorns wrapped around my arm like a sleeve, and as I gingerly tried to pull away, the skin tore, and the few berries I was clutching dropped to the ground.

As I continued walking, feeling the sting of scratches on my arm, I recalled how quickly I was trapped by the thicket when I extended my grasp. It reminded me of how easily all those unhealthy attachments grab at our psyches and take hold—addictions to busyness and food or compulsive behavior like the need to control and possess. They are reminiscent of the seed that falls among the briars and thorns and is suffocated.

The result is painful. When certain desires control our lives, they limit our freedom to love. We become more and more self-involved, and there is less room for relationships. We are also aware, on some level, that pursuing these desires will not bring us happiness, yet we continue. We return to them again and again, knowing full well that they will leave us feeling as if we have betrayed ourselves.

The gospel calls us to empty ourselves, but we struggle mightily. The bottom line is that we want to respond to God's love but cannot; we are flawed human beings. We easily become entangled and assume that the spiritual path is too demanding and should be left to those more diligent or graced than we are. No wonder that words like "detachment," "emptying," "releasing," "letting go," and "self-denial" are so difficult to discuss and so readily the source of misinterpretation and fear.

Where do we begin? From John of the Cross, we learn that our personal experience of God's love can affect us profoundly and inspire a transformation process; love itself fires the will so that we can do our part in freeing the heart. In the end, we discover freedom, an inner spaciousness that allows us to love God, others, and creation in the way they were meant to be loved.

This invitation to self-denial arises not only in our relationship with the divine but in any maturing love relationship; we are inspired to sacrifice for the sake of the one who has stolen our heart. We willingly release self-interest and accept emptying if love is at stake. This insight has helped me whenever I struggle with letting go. I recall how God first loved me in a personal way and how this love is the only love that can satisfy the human heart. St. Paul has the same insight in his Letter to the Philippians: "For him [Jesus Christ] I have accepted the loss of all other things, and look on them all as filth if only I can gain Christ" (3:8). This language of Paul, echoed by John of the

Cross, may sound radical, but it is simply the expression of a person who has fallen in love with the One who matters most.

MAKE A CHOICE

By finding satisfaction and strength in this love, it will have the courage and constancy to readily deny all other appetites. (Ascent I.14.2)

The gospel truth that the path of inner growth is narrow and will have to include sacrifice is central for growth in love (Matthew 7:13-14). This sacrifice of self happens not by accident but only by choice. However, John was well aware that a person must first have a healthy self-esteem in order to make this choice, for how can we give up something we do not possess? It follows that those who do not believe they are loved have every right to fear self-denial.

How do we make a choice? Not from a sense of obligation or duty imposed on us by the expectations of others, but from the openheartedness and strength we receive in the experience of God's love. Aware of the fullness of divine love, the will comes alive and finds the resolve to free the heart from obstacles. Trusting in this love, we are led beyond selfishness. Trust heals brokenness and guides us toward the right choices even when our sin is great: "God is never absent," John assures us, "not even from a soul in mortal sin" (*Canticle* 1.8).

Can we truly accept that by its very nature, love has the power to transform the heart? It helps to consider how human relationships develop and the way two people become involved in mutual sacrifice for the sake of love. Without the sacrifice, the relationship withers and eventually becomes quarrelsome and divisive. With an ongoing willingness to give oneself for the sake of the beloved, however, love flourishes. As we have seen, John had the example of his father's love to guide him. Certainly, the sacrifice of inheritance and prestige that his father made to his mother for the sake of their union in marriage influenced John throughout his life with each choice he made to give his heart away, and served as an example of the possibilities of authentic love.

Love also has the power to transform us because in loving deeply, we discover how human we truly are. Love tests us, and in doing so uncovers illusions, fears, insecurities, past hurts, and immaturity—in other words, our human woundedness. Who has explored love and not found their limitations exposed? What do we do with this pain? Protect ourselves?

John would suggest that we take to heart our inability to act freely and our incapacity to hand over our lives completely. Such self-knowledge introduces humility. With love we can no longer accept our self-image blindly and without reflection because "all the soul's infirmities are brought to light; they are set before its eyes to be felt and healed . . . just as dampness of a log of wood was unknown until fire applied to it made it sweat and smoke and sputter" (*Flame* 1.21, 22). John loved this image of a log of wood and used it frequently. He compares the soul to wood that remains unaware until it encounters fire. At first it smolders, revealing just how damp it is. Eventually, though, the fire transforms the log into itself; the soul becomes flame, and all its activities issue from this intense fire of union with the divine.

It is clear that making choices to love takes courage and a willingness to risk our very selves. The choices themselves are acts of love, not simply a testing ground or the initiation that a beginner must pass through in order to find success in the future. We are not waiting for the right moment to declare our love but are doing it all along. Making these choices each day in small and hidden ways, we are learning to say, "Everything I do I do with love, and everything I suffer I suffer with the delight of love" (*Canticle* 28.8).

LIKE LITTLE CHILDREN

It is plain that the appetites are wearisome and tiring. They resemble little children, restless and hard to please, always whining to their mother for this thing or that, and never satisfied. (Ascent I.6.6)

John uses the image of little children to make a point about the nature of unruly desires because, like children, they have the ability to cause chaos and weary our spirits. Anyone who has taken young children shopping knows the struggle that ensues. Children have no boundaries, so they grab everything within reach and insist on having whatever catches their attention. They have no discretion; the pleasure principle rules. Parents quickly grow tired of reigning in their petulant children.

When they act out of self-gratification, adults in relationship, whether in relationship with God or with others, are like children. The relationship is about them and their needs. When things do not meet their expectations, they become surly and condemning; they judge and snap at others, attempting to manipulate or control situations to suit their ends. They wear themselves out pursuing goals that will never make them happy. The result is that their relationships do not grow, and self-involvement effectively isolates them from others.

Children by nature are also shortsighted; they concentrate on immediate pleasure. Adults who act this way are interested in finding fulfillment in experiences that can never provide more than a temporary escape: alcohol, codependent relationships, food, and material possessions. When these experiences falter and eventually fail under the weight of expectation, they do not lead to self-reflection but to pursuing new diversions.

It is one thing, of course, to see these "childish" characteristics in others, but when we see them in ourselves, perhaps at a time of stress due to a setback in our lives, it can be a wake-up call. Losses, especially as we grow older, awaken us to our inability to find happiness and show us how deeply we share in the brokenness of the human condition. Feelings of pain that we may have tried to deny or hide from for so long begin to surface, and the heart calls out for healing and liberation. Only now do we understand how disordered our love for God and others has been. From the depths of our heart, we long for the freedom to love, and acknowledging our own incapacity to direct our lives, we surrender to the guidance of a love greater than ourselves.

In Leo Tolstoy's novelette *The Death of Ivan Ilyich*, Ivan finds himself unexpectedly on his deathbed. He has received an appointment as a judge in Moscow, and while hanging drapes in his new apartment in preparation for the arrival of his wife and children, he falls from a ladder, hitting his side. The pain grows worse until it is obvious that no medical treatment can provide a remedy and that he will die. As he lies in bed, he reviews his life, a life that he justified because he was simply responding to the expectations of others and upholding the values of society. But now he realizes that it was all an illusion, and he cries out in pain that is both moral and physical: "What if my entire life, my entire conscious life, simply was not the real thing?"[9] This dramatic upheaval awakens a deeper, more authentic self, freeing him to enjoy a new vision of light and truth. He reaches out to his wife and children in a gesture of love moments before he dies.

The Ascent

The first part, the night of senses, resembles early evening, that time of twilight when things begin to fade from sight. (Ascent I.2.5)

I once had the opportunity to climb one of the mountains in the Needles Range of Colorado. It was a beautiful sunny day, and as I stood at the foot of the mountain, the landscape seemed ethereal, buzzing with early morning light. The trail meandered invitingly through a meadow and then gently pushed upward. I was enthusiastic about the prospect of an easy climb.

As I hiked, I heard a mountain stream crashing over rocks nearby and became mesmerized by the sound. All around me the crimson of Indian paintbrush danced in the breeze. It wasn't long, though, before the climb became more rigorous, and I felt dizzy and unable to catch my breath. I had to sit down. It was humbling to realize that I was climbing too fast and had not allowed myself time to acclimate. Sometime later, when I finally approached the top of the mountain, I was greeted by an enormous slab of rock jutting into the sky. There was no more foliage, not even scrub trees, but only rock sculpted by the elements. The beautiful surroundings of the early climb had given way to a stark, primordial environment.

I took some time to rest and enjoy the wide expanse of blue sky and wandering clouds, but I soon became alarmed because in the distance I saw a thunderstorm suddenly gathering force. It seemed to appear out of nowhere, a threatening dark mass in a placid open sky. As the lightning and rain approached, I searched for cover near an overhang but quickly moved into the open when I realized that the solid rock could become a lightning rod. Thankfully, the storm passed quickly, leaving me shaken and sober. I realized again that I had misjudged the demands of the climb. I was naïve and unprepared.

This physical climb is much like the spiritual one that John describes in his treatise *The Ascent of Mount Carmel*. Those who begin the spiritual path do not quite recognize what they are getting themselves into; they may be mesmerized by the good feelings at the onset of the journey but do not expect the extent of the sacrifice, the dark night that awaits them. John of the Cross, however, stands at the top of the mountain as a wise guide who has experienced the climb and is eager to share his wisdom. His voice echoes through the rocky corridors, cautioning us to take our time, let go of distractions, be attentive, and trust the call of love.

This mountain ascent that introduces the dark night is at first an experience of dusk, but it will eventually lead into the utter darkness of contemplative faith. Of course, the night is not the final story; it opens into the dawn of new life. John calls the night at this stage "active" because it demands a good deal of our participation and demonstrates, through our willingness to incorporate a discipline into our lives, our commitment to take the inner way seriously. Though in itself the ascent is not a way of prayer, it is necessary groundwork for growth in prayer. Often, when prayer dries up, it is not because God has abandoned us but because we have taken our prayer life for granted, forgetting that love grows only through sacrifice.

The call of love that leads us into the night involves letting go of sinful attachments. But it also invites restraint from ordinary pleasures that lock us into a pattern of security, comfort, and eventually forgetfulness of what really matters—our relationship with God and others. This discipline is difficult to embrace in a culture that decries any restriction as a loss of personal freedom and insists that all our desires be met. To find solid footing in the ascent, we need to take a moment and ask ourselves, "What behaviors are hindering my growth as a loving person at this time in my life? What is the spirit of love calling me to change in my relationship with God and others?" In answering these questions, it is important not to push for answers but to be patient and live with the questions, allowing the Spirit to be our guide.

John's point is that when the initial joy and enthusiasm in our relationship with God begin to wane, previous attachments that were set aside will now come forward and clamor for our attention. Preferences for special foods and drink, favorite places to sit, chatting, different forms of entertainment, and numerous other ways of favoring and comforting ourselves begin to smother a burgeoning inner life. It is important to recognize that John is not interested in denying natural appetites like eating or drinking or even in judging the way they so easily distract our attention; this is part of being human. He focuses on attachments that, although perhaps insignificant at first glance, have over time rooted themselves in our hearts and minds like weeds and have the power to choke out new life. For example, we may find that our dependence on a particular food or beverage has become so strong over time that it has the power to disrupt our routine of work and prayer. We have to have a particular soft drink, for example, and find that the thought of it controls our attention. We realize that we need to abstain but may rationalize that food and drink are small matters and can do little harm.

John advises that we take even these small attachments seriously if they have become habitual. In the darkness of faith, we need to cut them loose in order to have the freedom to give ourselves to God. If we continue to let these desires sap our spirits, they will leave us feeling empty and desolate, cold toward others, and disinterested in the spiritual life. The truth is that we know we have chosen to displace energy that should be directed toward a relationship with God.

This discipline of the active night of the senses also involves being wary of visions, voices, and unusual experiences that can rise into our consciousness with surprising force. John, along with the spiritual teachers of the Christian tradition, makes it clear that "signs and wonders" can mislead us. That's because good or evil forces can be the source of such experiences, and we need guidance to know whether the visions and voices are attempts to deceive us. This is an important issue today, since many look for signs to boost their faith rather than focusing their attention on the Mystery toward which the signs point. John of the Cross cautions, "We should pay no heed to them, but be only interested in directing the will, with fortitude, toward God" (*Ascent* II.29.12). His position is that we should not look to signs because everything we need is already revealed in Christ.

There is no holding back in this climb; it takes our full participation. We make the choice with our entire being to redirect our desires for the sake of love. Yet at the same time, we acknowledge that the ascent is only possible because grace has led us to the mountain and continues to support us. At first the experience of "darkness" is unsettling because it involves voluntary restraint when it comes to the "good things" in our lives—pleasures that in the past we did not recognize as harmful but that have begun to imprison our hearts. Eventually, however, love gains momentum and attachments simply hold less power over us; they fade into the twilight because our eyes are turned toward a stronger glow—the light of divine love.

MOUNT CARMEL

Oh, if spiritual persons knew how much spiritual good and abundance they lose by not attempting to raise their appetites above childish things. (*Ascent* I.5.4)

John sketched Mount Carmel for the nuns at Beas as a summary of his treatise *The Ascent of Mount Carmel.* The mountain had three dark lines that represented paths to the top. The two side paths were detours; the middle one was the path of perfection.

The middle path invited the person to reject attachment to all desires so that nothing would make him weary or divert him from his goal of God alone. Below the mountain was a series of *"nadas"* that directed the spiritual journey. As John writes,

> To reach satisfaction in all
> desire its possession in nothing.
> To come to possess all
> desire the possession of nothing.
> To arrive at being all
> desire to be nothing.
> To come to the knowledge of all
> desire the knowledge of nothing. (*Ascent* I.13.11)

The focus is on *nada* (nothing) for the sake of *todo* (all). Nada is the process of discovering freedom by releasing handicaps to personal growth. This journey into the night consists of ridding ourselves of harmful behavior and self-centered pleasure seeking.

As we have seen, the journey is initiated by God, but we are not bystanders; we play our part with the choices we make. Of course, following this path puts us at odds with cultural values, but this in itself is a taste of darkness. Some may back away from this guidance because it is too strict to become a way of life. John, however, does not propose an ongoing asceticism. Instead, this is preparatory discipline, a necessary first step in training the will. In the same way that a serious athlete will have to spend some time in rigorous training for a major event, so we, too, need to prepare. Once this initial stage of discipline runs its course, it will leave in its wake a stronger will for the journey ahead.

John's spiritual counsel may also ring harsh to modern ears because we feel he is negating our passion for human dignity and the goodness of creation. This seems true until we remember that he was guided by the experience of love. He did not negate the value of human dignity or the inherent goodness of the created world—in fact, he celebrated both. John insisted that human beings were created in the image and likeness of God and out of love for union with God. He also believed that the world reflected infinite beauty, and anyone who contemplated it participated in divine love: "Since creatures gave the soul signs of her Beloved and showed within themselves traces of his beauty and excellence, love grew in her" (*Canticle* 6.2). Images of creation abound in John's poetry, and he regarded all creation as the image of Jesus Christ.

So then why the harsh tone? If he was not interested in taking away the things we enjoy in favor of a radical ascent to spiritual heights, then what was he emphasizing? John had no problem with everyday pleasures but rather with the cravings of the heart, the desire to have something simply because we want it: "For we are not discussing the mere lack of things; this lack will not divest the soul if it craves for all these objects" (*Ascent* I.3.4). He recognized, as do we when we acknowledge our addictive tendencies, how easily attachment to the good things of this world can get out of control and fuel our desires. As a result, we see the physical world, not as a gift (in which case we would seek to protect the dignity of the planet and treat it with care), but as something that should suit us. In the end, it is not the world that must be put aside but the seductive pull of self-centered desires, which give us the illusion of self-sufficiency and godlike control.

John speaks of the nothingness of creation when he says, "All creatures of heaven and earth are nothing when compared to God" (*Ascent* I.4.3). But in doing so, he underscores a fundamental truth: God is the source of all creation, and nothing exists without the light of God's love. The urgency and strictness in his tone come from his insistence that ultimately, we cannot waste time allowing our lives to be centered on anything other than God. God alone is the source of happiness; all else is secondary.

Given John's mystical experience of the infinite beauty and goodness that pervade the cosmos, how could we expect him to compromise the reality of God's love? Wouldn't our attitude change if we experienced the same vision, even if only in a flash? Wouldn't our mundane routine be transformed if we trusted that divine love was a fundamental reality and always present? What would happen if on an ordinary day, while you were preparing peanut-butter-and-jelly sandwiches for your children, you suddenly found yourself immersed in light, as this author did?

> The entire room became luminous and so alive with movement that everything seemed suspended—yet pulsating—for an instant, like light waves. Intense joy swelled inside me, and my immediate response was gratitude—gratitude for everything, every tiny thing in that space. The shelter of the room became a warm embrace; water flowing from the tap seemed a tremendous miracle; and my children became, for a moment, not my progeny or charges or my tasks, but eternal beings of infinite singularity and complexity whom I would one day, in an age to come, apprehend in their splendid fullness.[10]

Wouldn't this experience move you to take a stand, insisting to others that only infinite love will satisfy the craving of the human heart and that all else inevitably falls short of our expectations?

FINDING REST

In this nakedness the spirit finds its quietude and rest. For in coveting nothing, nothing tires it. (Ascent I.13.13)

Which is more important, the pursuit of happiness or the pursuit of freedom? John chose freedom because he understood that because of original sin, we do not see clearly. Rather, we must contend with a multitude of illusions that distort our vision and hide the truth. We consistently choose what we think will bring us happiness and instead find disappointment and personal suffering. And even when we uncover the source of happiness, we discover that our will is too weak to pursue it.

In the opening paragraph of his autobiography, *The Seven Storey Mountain*, Thomas Merton looks back on his gift of freedom, inherited at birth: "I came into the world free by nature, in the image of God; I was nevertheless the prisoner of my own violence and my own selfishness, in the image of the world into which I was born."[11] During his youth, Merton pursued the freedom to do what he pleased and did not like the person he had become. Eventually, after his conversion to Catholicism at the age of twenty-six, he recognized that true freedom can only be found within ourselves and is cultivated by recognizing our unhealthy attachment to what is not God.

For John, the whole purpose for redirecting our desires toward God alone is not to impose an external discipline that weighs down the spirit but rather to release the true center of the heart, the true self that hungers to be free. On the one hand, this release requires sacrifice and the ability to say no to the image of self that we have created and that has prevented communion with others and God. On the other hand, it requires the willingness to say yes to the spirit of love imprisoned within us, the self in Christ. In the end, authentic transformation is not, as I once thought, willfully rejecting old ways and replacing them with new ones, but openness to the touch of divine love that recreates us. We learn to release control repeatedly, handing our lives over to God so that we can be created into something entirely new.

As a wise spiritual guide, John recognizes that the beginning of any journey is difficult, and our choice to turn toward divine love must be wholehearted or not at all. We cannot at the same time move toward the divine and yet accommodate our own interests. Authentic spiritual growth will not allow us to make our lives partially available. Love demands total presence. Our entire being—actions, thoughts, emotions, and secret desires— was created for completion in God. To think that we can parcel out pieces of ourselves to be transformed while continuing to shape a comfortable self-image undermines this reality.

The difficulty is that we think of our hearts as open, pliable, and ready to change, but in reality, says the prophet Jeremiah, they are hard and stubborn. "Can the Ethiopian change his skin, or the leopard his spots?" Jeremiah asks. "And you, can you do right, being so accustomed to wrong?" (13:23). In time, with greater self-knowledge and deeper awareness of our own weaknesses, failures, and inadequacies, we see that any change—even a small change—is truly a gift. At first we practice submitting our lives fully to God's hands through everyday events, insights, and relationships; eventually, with the help of grace, we release even our investment in changing ourselves.

Each of us, in our heart of hearts, bears the image of Christ who waits to take form as beauty, simplicity, and poverty. And each of us will make a choice—yes or no—to place our lives completely in the hands of God, to be molded into an expression of transcendent beauty. After all, "We are God's work of art, created in Christ Jesus for the good works which God has already designated to make up our way of life" (Ephesians 2:10).

It bears repeating that John does not propose a strict asceticism that demands tremendous effort on our part. He had experimented with this approach in his youth and found that it easily got out of hand; asceticism became an end in itself. Rather, he believes in the call of love that draws us to God, and emphasizes that ascetic practices should reinforce a disposition to sacrifice for the sake of love.

For John, the soul is like a bird that needs to be released so that it can fly. Whatever holds it back means it cannot fly freely. Watch birds at a bird feeder, and you will marvel at their simplicity, freedom, and beauty in flight. This is the freedom that is waiting to be released within us. But just as a small thread can keep us from flying, John tells us, even an insignificant attachment can weigh down the soul: "It makes little difference whether a bird is tied by a thin thread or a cord" (*Ascent* I.11.4). His point is not that we should be pursuing an idealized state of perfection in which all attachments are eliminated;

this would deny our human limitations. Who can even imagine this state of perfection?

Rather, John is attempting to emphasize the fact that even small attachments can accumulate and lead to great ones. So even if an attachment to a particular food, feeling, or thing seems insignificant at first, it can eventually undermine our ability to give ourselves fully in love. How can the heart even consider giving itself fully if it secretly covets an attachment and is unwilling to release it? John witnessed people he guided on the spiritual path being held back by things they could not release. The negative effect is twofold: "What is worse, not only do they fail to advance, but they turn back because of their small attachment, losing what they gained on their journey" (*Ascent* I.11.5).

The love that inspires the journey of freedom, the love that accepts us as children of God with a divine destiny, is a love nurtured by friendship with Christ. John has no intention of leading us toward a joyless spirituality but rather to a life of freedom in Christ. This life is not one of inner tension and sullenness but of peace and joy. John describes this freedom in *The Dark Night*:

In darkness and secure,
By the secret ladder, disguised,
—ah, the sheer grace!—
In darkness and concealment,
my house being now all stilled. (stanza 2)

Walking with God

Take God for your bridegroom and friend, and walk with him continually; and you will not sin and will learn to love, and the things you must do will work out prosperously for you. (Sayings 68)

How can we begin to redirect our desires toward God? John suggests simply that we walk in the presence of God.

This may seem like an exercise of the imagination that will be difficult to practice in our busy lives, but for John, it is a vital act of faith. No matter where we are or what we are doing, we are *in* God. At first we may imagine that Christ walks alongside us during the day, but eventually our faith journey leads us to discover the spirit of Christ alive in our hearts beyond any image, thought, or feeling.

Walking in the presence of God runs contrary to our usual experience of getting though the day. Through the regular course of our days, we often create an illusory reality that centers on our own desires and forgets the fundamental ground of love. Forgetfulness seems to be our ongoing human condition and is reinforced by familiar rhythms that protect our security and comfort, including the things that draw us into addictive behaviors. Because of this forgetfulness, however, we find ourselves feeling isolated—removed from God, others, and creation. Love falters; our ability to hand ourselves over in love diminishes.

However, the practice of walking with God and giving God our loving attention throughout the day empties the self and creates space for love. I once saw a documentary in which Blessed

Mother Teresa was interviewed by a British journalist. As the camera panned the scene, it showed Mother Teresa holding a small circle of wooden beads behind her back, fingering each in turn, as she answered the interviewer's questions. Who can guess what words she repeated in her heart? What caught my attention, however, was the natural way in which she forgot herself and remained in touch with the divine, even in a formal setting.

There is no room for self-posturing when we realize how profoundly we are embraced by love. This is the gospel path: Knowing ourselves loved by God, we find the will to forget ourselves and live in communion with God, others, and creation. In losing ourselves and leaving behind our old ways, we allow ourselves to be emptied, creating "heart space" so that we can be filled. "The one who walks in the love of God seeks neither gain nor reward, but seeks only to lose with the will all things and self for God" (*Canticle* 29.11). In the end, we find fullness of life in Christ and freedom for the kingdom of God.

In the next chapter, we turn our attention to the center of our journey toward divine union: Jesus Christ. The healing power of Christ's resurrection has given each one of us the grace to become a new person in Christ—a person at peace, a person empowered by authentic freedom and no longer controlled by external things. From this deep sense of inner peace, we trust Jesus to guide us beyond the limitations of our own nature into the possibilities of the spiritual life and the fullness of prayer.

Suggestions for Reflection

1. What baggage might you be carrying now that prevents you from facing yourself honestly and growing in love?

2. Looking over the activities and spirituality of your daily life, where do you see the call arising to let go of attachments? How do you feel called to respond?

3. How does this counsel from John apply to you at this point in your life: "To come to enjoy what you have not / you must go by a way in which you enjoy not" (*Ascent* I.13.11)?

4. Without the self-knowledge gained through reflecting on your life and actions, called an "examen of consciousness," it is difficult to change behaviors. How often do you take time to be open and receptive to the voice of God within you? In what ways do you find yourself challenged to respond to the Spirit of love today? How have you begun to integrate wisdom gained from self-reflection into your choices and decisions?

CHAPTER THREE

DRAWN TO CHRIST

Christ is mine and all for me.
—*Sayings of Light and Love*, 27

There is much to fathom in Christ, for he is like an abundant mine with many recesses of treasures, so that however deep individuals may go they never reach the end or bottom, but rather in every recess find new veins with new riches everywhere.
—*The Spiritual Canticle*, 37.4

During a group discussion on prayer, I was surprised to hear how many individuals were either using the Jesus Prayer in their daily lives or were attracted to it. I remember one person in particular talking about how the prayer gave her an ongoing sense of Jesus' presence that was so pervasive that it guided her through the difficult experience of losing her father.

It was apparent to the group that repeating the name of Jesus (using a short form, either "Jesus" or "Jesus, have mercy," or a longer form, "Jesus, have mercy on me, a sinner") was not simply a pious gesture or spiritual exercise but invoked his real presence. To repeat Jesus' name opened their hearts to his energy. Each person in the group who employed the prayer acknowledged that it had changed their lives and their relationship with God.

John of the Cross, too, shares this passion for the energy of Jesus, this spark of love that ignites the heart. Jesus Christ is the center, the primal source of energy. Though our own relationship with Jesus may have become static and one-dimensional, John invites us to take a deeper look and discover something dynamic, contagious, and mysterious. In the process of getting to know Jesus, we discover a deeper sense of ourselves and are drawn into a deepening prayer.

Also, it is through Christ that we find the strength to let go of that inauthentic self, that part of us that is caught up in a multitude of desires. In order to realize this goal, John emphasizes, we must follow Christ. That flame within us guides us toward seeking not ourselves but God, and our growing love for Christ gives us the motivation to rid ourselves of the desires and ways of living that close off our relationship with God. Christ is the perfect model of divine love, and in becoming more like him, we uncover an expansive love in our lives.

If a life of faith is a journey into the darkness, then it is faith directed to Christ who is light. Christ as light is a central image in the Gospel of John. As a person becomes more open to this loving knowledge, he or she receives the gift of wisdom and union with God.

What kind of prayer does a relationship with Jesus involve? At first it is a prayer that appeals to our imagination and reason, like a prayer of repetition, such as the Jesus Prayer, or a prayer in which we ponder a passage from the Scriptures, like *lectio divina*. Eventually, with the help of grace, it becomes a prayer of silence without images or reflection. It is a prayer that contemplates Jesus simply and lovingly, like Mary, who willingly stopped her activity to rest in Jesus' presence while her sister, Martha, made preparations for their guest. In this prayer of silence, or contemplative prayer, we attend to or "hear" the eternal silence of the Word poured forth eternally from God. John's intention is to awaken us to this Word that God speaks in silence at the center of our lives.

Let us begin by taking a closer look at the importance John placed on a relationship with Christ, and then explore how this relationship evolves into deeper prayer.

Christ as Gift

The first thing the soul desires on coming to the vision of God is to know and enjoy the deep secrets and mysteries of the Incarnation and the ancient ways of God dependent on it. (Canticle 37.1)

Mystics have a way of placing ancient truths in a new light. They present for us what we already believe but in a way that fills us with wonder and awe, as if we were seeing it for the first time. John's passion for the Incarnation is one example, as he introduces us to what may be possible if we are truly in love with God.

Imagine waking up in the morning to the touch or kiss of a loved one. You find yourself rising gently from the depths of the unconscious, like a sailor finally reaching home after wandering distant and foreign shores. In comparison, what is it like to awaken to the "kiss" of divine love in the depths of the heart? St. Bernard of Clairvaux, referring to the first line of the Song of Songs, describes God's kiss as a secret expression of ineffable love that brings us back to life. According to Bernard, the kiss surpasses anything known in the physical world, and represents the intimate touch of the spirit of Christ.[12]

Who can begin to describe the depth and meaning of the intimate touch of the spirit of Christ on our hearts? We know Jesus Christ as the fullness of God's revelation to humanity, but we often bracket this as a dogmatic truth rather than looking upon it as God's personal self-disclosure to us. In other words, God has entered into human experience and has given us in the Person of Jesus a glimpse into divine love. Divine love is so ready and willing to have an intimate relationship with us that it actually becomes one of us in order to reveal itself more. John reminds us that in Jesus Christ, God holds back nothing; he reveals the compassionate depths of divine nature by dying for us on the cross and rising from the dead, holding out the hope that we, too, will one day be transformed.

John was amazed that the Father offered us the gift of his Son, that God became human in Christ: "For this is how God loved the world: he gave his only Son" (John 3:16). It was a gift, he believed, given to each one of us personally. To truly understand John's teaching, each of us has to claim our fundamental giftedness, namely, that Christ belongs to me and my unique personal history. God not only knows my thoughts, feelings, and experiences but identifies with them in the Person of Jesus Christ, who has become like us in all things but sin (Hebrews 4:15).

When the Word touches our hearts with his personal presence, when we are "kissed" by him, we really know God and are in communion with the divine. Only in the depths of our hearts is the Word fully revealed to us. Imagining Jesus in the Incarnation or on the cross is not enough. The incarnate

Word is more than visible and tangible to us; he is a sign and invitation calling us to open ourselves to a fuller experience of revelation, to the divine presence within us. Only by an inner experience of grace—the touch of the Word's own presence—can we really know Jesus and, in knowing him, know the Father as well.

If we are looking for God to intervene in our lives or for miracles to guide us, then our faith is limited. The faith that Jesus desires, insists John, is the total surrender of ourselves to him so that he can reveal himself intimately to us. According to John, Jesus knows what is in our hearts and will not reveal himself to us if our hearts are not open to his presence. What God wants to communicate to us cannot be expressed externally or in words; it can be expressed only in our awakening to the touch of a loving presence.

Trust, then, that everything is given to us through the Word made flesh, and we need nothing more. This overflowing of the Father's love transforms us and all of creation. The more we immerse ourselves in the mystery of the Incarnation, the more wisdom we will gain to appreciate the beauty and goodness within ourselves, in others, and in the world at large. John himself saw light everywhere, in the faces of the people he met and in the forms of the natural world, all of which he believed were an extension of his love for Christ.

Once I take the Incarnation personally and accept that God gave his only Son especially for me, then I look at the world around me and see everything in a dramatically different way: It is all given through Christ. My vision changes; my eyes are renewed. In wonder I see the physical world, from quarks to the cosmos, as an expression of the Word made flesh, God's love taking form.

Friendship with Christ

Have a habitual desire to imitate Christ in all your deeds. (*Ascent* I.13.3)

Where do we begin if we are drawn to a relationship with Christ? If we are serious about answering this question, we need to move slowly and cautiously and depend on the guidance of others. For John, the fundamental issue in spiritual growth is whether we have the desire to bring our lives into conformity with Christ's. At the beginning of the spiritual path, some may want to imitate Christ, but it is just talk; their actual response is weak. Others who are truly drawn to a relationship with Christ will want to know Christ better and be willing to sacrifice whatever is necessary to make their desires and attitudes Christ's own.

Imitation of Christ is not simply a spiritual exercise on our agenda. The desire to bring our lives into conformity with Christ goes to the center of who we are; by discovering who Christ is, we discover our true self. This is a lifelong journey that involves an ongoing growth in relationship with the truth of our lives.

If we take friendship with Christ seriously, it will require work because every serious relationship requires work. We cannot wish the relationship into existence. This work is daunting because we realize it will change the whole of our lives and will necessarily include sacrifice. If our desire to conform our lives to Christ is to mature, we need to let go of our own disordered desires and attitudes because "this death is patterned on Christ's for he is our model and light" (*Ascent* II.7.9). In short, this work means choosing the cross because Christ, who is our Way, experienced the suffering and abandonment of Calvary, showing us what it means to die for love.

What better example of conforming one's life to Christ than that of St. Thérèse of Lisieux, who was fearless when it came to protecting her friendship with Jesus. She translated John of the Cross' counsel of detachment into a simple path that she called the "Little Way." To remain true to this path, she took every opportunity in her day-to-day life to practice humility and charity—helping those who showed little gratitude, choosing menial jobs that others refused, and celebrating the good fortune of others gracefully. She felt that these little victories, which remained "hidden," pleased Jesus more than greater deeds that could attract more attention. In Thérèse's example, we find an avenue for following Jesus that can appeal to many today because it gives attention to the small challenges that all of us face in our ordinary routines of life. Thérèse's path is also simple and concrete enough for anyone to follow.

SHARING OUR LIVES WITH CHRIST

Study his life in order to know how to imitate him. (*Ascent* I.13.3)

Getting to know Jesus on more than a surface level will mean talking with him as a friend, sharing our lives with him, eventually hearing his voice in our hearts. Our prayer involves reflecting on the life of Christ and the mysteries of faith, which is called "discursive meditation." This prayer not only strengthens faith but shows God that we are serious about changing our lives.

The groundwork for this prayer involves immersion in Scripture. We can read Scripture at arm's length, simply for occasional inspiration, or we can read it intimately as food for the soul. If it is the latter, then we find ourselves moving slowly from one scene or idea to another, taking the time to ponder each one, letting the words and images sink into the heart. Just as we take time to taste good food and wine, we need to appreciate and ingest the words of Scripture.

John was in the habit of carrying a Bible when he traveled or reading it when he found free time in the monastery garden. He pondered Scripture and let it draw him into contemplation. He even sang when the Spirit moved him. Particular images would catch his attention and resonate in his heart, so he lingered with them and allowed them to draw his heart to Christ throughout the day.

As we read the Bible, not only do we discover information about Christ, but we find ourselves attracted to aspects of Jesus' life, attitudes, and values. A growing loving relationship develops, and we become less interested in the attachments that hinder this relationship. We desire to be like Christ—in other words, to take on his Spirit and do the will of the Father in every aspect of our lives. To see the Father's will as Christ did means dedicating our entire lives to the glory of God.

This kind of reading invites us to compare our own attitudes, values, and desires with Christ's. The challenge is to make

Christ's perspective our own. At first we may become discouraged, thinking that we could never attain the ideal to which the gospels call us. We may even find the words we read difficult to relate to in our own lives. John tells us that the words of Scripture do not fire the heart until our lives are less disordered. Until then, "Those who do not have a sound palate, but seek other tastes, cannot taste the spirit and life of God's words; his words, rather, are distasteful to them" (*Flame* 1.5).

John's approach to reading Scripture makes good sense when we think of it in terms of *lectio divina*, a way of reading Scripture handed down through the centuries. In the practice of lectio. or "sacred reading," it is less about our reading and more about our willingness to allow our lives to be read, that is, to be pried open by the loving and merciful hand of God. Lectio involves reading slowly and reflectively, stopping when we find a passage that speaks to us and letting that passage, phrase, or story enter into our own heart. We reflect on the passage in relation to our own life, let our reflection draw us into a verbal prayer or song, and then spend time in the silent presence of God.

Implicit in any practice of meditative prayer is our willingness to surrender again and again to the work of God in and through our lives. Without this desire to open our hearts, prayer will fail. We know this from experience. Meditation shows God that we are serious about changing our lives and are willing to be nourished by faith. The emotional satisfaction we receive with this form of prayer feeds the soul of the beginner and readies it for a more mature relationship.

Suffering with Jesus

The journey, then, does not consist in consolations, delights, and spiritual feelings, but in the living death of the cross, sensory and spiritual, exterior and interior. (Ascent II.7.11)

John is quick to remind us that our prayer journey will not always fulfill our expectation of good feelings and spiritual comfort but will soon become the way of the cross.

The image of the cross appeared unexpectedly to John during his own prayer when he was chaplain to the nuns of the Convent of the Incarnation in Ávila from 1574 to 1577. He responded by sketching Christ on the cross, which is described in this way:

The sketch is of Christ crucified hanging in space, turned toward his people, and seen from a new perspective. The cross is erect. The body, lifeless and contorted, with the head bent over, hangs forward so that the arms are held only by the nails. Christ is seen from above, from the view of the Father. He is more worm than man, weighed down by the sins of human beings, leaning toward the world for which he died.[13]

This sketch of the cross etched itself in John's heart during his imprisonment in Toledo, which lasted for nine months, beginning in December 1577. The pain and isolation that he experienced at the hands of his community allowed him to live the cross in a way that he perhaps had never imagined. Out of this anguish, though, came not despair but the poetry of *The Spiritual Canticle*. The cross for him was not about suffering; it became an entrance into new life.

John envisioned himself as a prophet called to proclaim the cross as a way of transformation and passionate love. We can imagine that his calling began at an early age with the poverty suffered by his family upon his father's death. As a boy, John also saw human suffering while working in a hospital. He depended on patronage for his education and later chose to live a religious life of austerity and privation. These exterior experiences of suffering, including his imprisonment, formed his spirit early on, but they cannot be compared to the inner desolation he would experience in his spiritual life, which he described in *The Ascent of Mount Carmel* and *The Dark Night*.

The image of the cross held great importance for John because Jesus followed the way of the cross. To choose Jesus, then, clearly means that we choose the cross, namely, self-denial. Of course, nothing could be more at odds with our modern culture, which encourages self-promotion. It is easier to choose the path of upward mobility for the sake of success and self-aggrandizement rather than the downward path of sacrifice for the sake of love.

Christ's experience of desolation and abandonment at Calvary shows us what it means to sacrifice for love and to rely completely on God alone. Jesus was not only stripped of his clothes but was exposed to a profound sense of abandonment, of utter separation from the Father. If we embrace Christ as our Way, then the path we follow is not one of self-interest but of selfless love. This presumes that because God is love, we trust that we are loved unconditionally. One who follows this path finds freedom and joy because there is no longer a self to defend and protect. We are free to walk in truth with Truth itself.

Christ tells us, "If anyone wants to be a follower of mine, let him renounce himself and take up his cross and follow me. Anyone who wants to save his life will lose it; but anyone who loses his life for my sake, and for the sake of the gospel, will save it" (Mark 8:34-35). At first glance this may seem like strident counsel, but John shows us that if you follow Christ's footsteps wholeheartedly, you realize that self-denial is not an end in itself but makes space for the joy of new life, for the resurrection. Being crucified with Christ is an experiential participation in the paschal mystery; it is death to the illusory image of self in order that the true self, the image of God, may rise with the resurrected Jesus. In the end, Christ promises followers not darkness but light, a love beyond anything this world has witnessed.

John reminds us that the cross represents an invitation to pattern our own lives on Christ—to die to that part of ourselves that prevents union with the love of God. He insists that spiritual comfort and relief at dark times is not as important as love. John would acknowledge that it is difficult to put into words the mystery of Calvary; however, he reaffirms that the cross, in all its harshness and radical simplicity, offers consolation to troubled souls even in the most difficult times. He writes simply, "If individuals resolutely submit to the carrying of the cross, if they decidedly want to find and endure trial in all things for God, they will discover in all of them great relief and sweetness" (*Ascent* II.7.7). The cross, representing the heart of Jesus on Calvary, does not take us away from this world but renews the human spirit in life, love, and hope, no matter the suffering.

Familiarity with John's experience and teaching prompts us to reflect on the image of the cross as seen through the prism of our personal history. Where do we find God encouraging growth in love through the transforming fire of suffering? What events have purified our souls so that we began to see ourselves and our lives differently, perhaps no longer as our own but as lived in Christ?

Suffering has a way of opening our eyes if we allow it. From the perspective of our vulnerability, we see ourselves and others differently, as humble human beings whose lives are sheer gift. Suffering also has the potential to deepen compassion, giving us the capacity to reach out to others in surprising ways. We witness this growth in humility and compassion both in our own lives and in the lives of friends and loved ones who have struggled to integrate a loss.

Water of Life

O spring like crystal! (*The Spiritual Canticle*, stanza 12)

While visiting a farm, I remember being asked to retrieve water from a spring nearby. I will never forget stepping down into a cool, dank cave, its walls dripping with moisture. The atmosphere, dark and mysterious, was so pervasive that the cave felt alive, like an extension of my skin. The earth itself was sweating and pouring forth life. I held an empty container under a bubbling stream, my eyes riveted by the clear liquid as it flowed along the path it had carved in the rock over the years. It was as if I were seeing water for the first time.

Water is a potent symbol in each of our lives, particularly at the beginning. We emerge from a moist womb into a dry environment, and we are submerged in water again at baptism. In the beginning, at least, our lives are more directly influenced by water than by earth, wind, or fire.

Early Carmelites—pilgrims who wanted to follow Christ—traced the footsteps of the prophet Elijah to Mount Carmel and established a dwelling place there. The mountain represented an oasis, a sanctuary where true pilgrims could find living water, that is, intimate union with God. Even today the Carmelite charism might be characterized as searching for living springs to fill the heart's deepest desire for spiritual refreshment.[14]

Pilgrims know that this journey to uncover water will always involve sacrifice. In the classic fable *The Little Prince*, a pilot loses control of his plane and drops into the Sahara desert. He encounters a small boy who talks of the possibilities of love, but the pilot is more interested in the practical difficulties of fixing his plane. When the boy, the little prince, invites him to search for a spring in the desert, the pilot hesitates. How could a spring be the answer to his predicament? Yet he decides reluctantly to accompany the little prince, and both of them walk deep into the desert interior, where they find a well bubbling with cool, life-giving water. Seeing the sunlight shimmer on the water, the pilot knows immediately that this water has been his heart's desire all along.

Desert experiences have a way of limiting our vision and increasing our concern, worry, and even anxiety. In graced moments, though, we find the capacity to trust that we are being taken by the hand and led out of a desert toward a living spring that exists at the center of our lives. We find sustenance in the psalmist's words: "The LORD is my light and my salvation; whom shall I fear?" (Psalm 27:1, NRSV).

The prophet Jeremiah called God "the fountain of living water" (Jeremiah 2:13). Christ took the opportunity at the side of the well to reveal to the Samaritan woman that he is the water of life (John 4:4-42). The woman had carried her empty clay pots—vessels that represented her parched and weary soul—to Jacob's well and found Jesus waiting. Was this merely a chance encounter? Can we not assume that Jesus wanted to address her personally and offer her the opportunity to refresh both her body and soul? At first she was confused by the promise of eternal water. But so was Nicodemus when Jesus told him that it was necessary to be "born through water and the Spirit" in order to enter the kingdom of heaven (3:5), and so are we when we become stubbornly fixated on the idea that the physical, practical reality is the only one that matters. However, Jesus' personal invitation struck the hardened core of the Samaritan woman's heart and tapped a secret wellspring of love that gushed up, bathing and healing her. She left her pots and returned to town with a new vision, telling everyone to come and see the One who revealed everything to her.

John of the Cross, too, thirsted for this eternal water of life; he wanted to immerse himself completely in union with Christ. He writes in *The Spiritual Canticle*,

O spring like crystal!
If only, on your silvered-over faces,
you would suddenly form

the eyes I have desired,
which I bear sketched deep within my heart. (stanza 12)

The "spring like crystal" in the poem represents the fountain of all life flowing toward God. From the time of our baptism, each of us participates, with the help of our faith, in this movement toward God. The source of the stream, however, remains hidden, "silvered-over," in the mysterious dark recesses of the inner self. God dwells in this darkness, and we long to peer into the depths.

Again, John was not satisfied with the "silvered-over" surface of the water. Led by the image of the crucified Christ etched in his heart, he pursued a face-to-face vision of Christ the Beloved, a union of love with the Beloved: "I lost myself, and was found" (*Canticle*, stanza 29).

Imagine two lovers gently gazing into each other's eyes. In the end, John's quest is the quest of all spiritual seekers who search out the depths of self, trusting that they already possess the treasure they seek. In the union of love with the Beloved, we discover what Paul meant when he wrote, "I live, now not I; but Christ lives in me" (see Galatians 2:20). Commenting on this passage, John writes, "In saying, 'I live, now not I,' he meant that even though he had life it was not his because he was transformed in Christ, and it was divine more than human" (*Canticle* 12.8).

At some point in our lives, we may wake up to the reality that our entire history is not our own but the history of Christ acted out through our lives. Our deepest self is the bubbling up of living water within us. At some point, we recognize that we were created for immersion in this eternal spring. Thomas Merton explores this idea in his poem "The Biography."

> Christ, from my cradle, I had known You everywhere,
> And even though I sinned, I walked in You, and knew
> You were my world:
> You were my France and England,
> My seas and my America:
> You were my life and air, and yet I would not own You.
>
> . . . .
>
> If on Your Cross Your life and death and mine are one,
> Love teaches me to read, in You, the rest of a new history.
> I trace my days back to another childhood. . . .
>
> Until I come again to my beginning,
> And find a manger, star and straw,
> A pair of animals, some simple men,
> And thus I learn that I was born,
> Now not in France, but Bethlehem.[15]

When we see ourselves in Christ, the day of our birth is not found on our birth certificate but in Bethlehem. Our dying is not limited to our individual times of suffering but is acted out on Calvary. What can we do but let our lives become a longing for immersion in the fertile water that is our life and a face-to-face vision of God?

SUGGESTIONS FOR REFLECTION

1. When were you drawn to Christ as a personal friend, and how did this affect your daily living? How would you describe your relationship with Christ today?

2. Immerse yourself in the following passage, savor it, and let it speak to your heart:

   I have been crucified with Christ and yet I am alive; yet it is no longer I, but Christ living in me. The life that I am now living, subject to the limitation of human nature, I am living in faith, faith in the Son of God who loved me and gave himself for me. (Galatians 2:19-20)

   Reflect on it, and then write a short prayer as your response. Finally, spend some time in silence, resting in Christ's presence.

3. John of the Cross advises following Jesus through study and prayer. If you are inclined, choose one of the four gospels for your morning prayer. Read a passage, letting a phrase or verse speak to you. Reflect on it and give your feelings expression in prayer. Finish with silence. Let your morning prayer influence you in the events that occur throughout your day.

CHAPTER FOUR

FROM MEDITATION TO CONTEMPLATION

A person likes to remain alone in loving
awareness of God, without particular considerations,
in interior peace and quiet.
—The Ascent of Mount Carmel, II.13.4

A touching story reveals much about John's perspective on prayer. Sr. Catalina de la Cruz, a humble, down-to-earth woman who was a cook for the community, wanted to know why the frogs jumped into the pool and hid at the bottom just before she approached them. John answered that they found peace and security in the depths at the center of the pool. Then he added, "That is what you must do: . . . plunge into the depth and center, which is God, hiding yourself in him."[16]

John would have our soul be like a rock, plummeting to the depths, surrendering completely to the weight of love. As it falls deeper and deeper, passing beyond all the impediments that hinder growth, it eventually hits deep center—the center of the earth—where it rests fully in union with God (*Flame* 1.13).

The most important thing is our attitude toward divine love, our willingness to give our lives over to love and let it become our guide into the depths. What is most important is not a technique of prayer but our attention toward the central energy, the divine inflow of love that is our life, for "love is the inclination, strength, and power for the soul in making its way to God, for love unites it with God" (*Flame* 1.13).

In the beginning, prayer arises out of our desire to remain in touch with divine love. It is more focused on us and our effort, as well as on the feeling we receive. We work at this prayer using images, reflection, or whatever it takes to redirect our attention to God.

Eventually, as our love relationship with God grows and we become more in touch with this divine presence, we simply want to rest at the center, becoming part of the flow of divine love, the "secret and peaceful and loving inflow of God" (*Dark Night* 1.10.6). Prayer in this case is fully dependent on grace, and much simpler. Why? Because it is God's work; God takes over. We simply free-fall into the depths and hide in God, trusting that this is where we will find peace, security, and communion with the divine.

This plunge into the deep, or contemplative prayer, is a dark night because we do not yet have the capacity to receive the fullness of divine love. The dark night expands our hearts, preparing our souls for intimacy with the divine. The gospels remind us that the path of prayer will not be easy; it is "a narrow gate and a hard road" (Matthew 7:14). However, the darkness is at the same time the inflow of divine love healing the soul, restoring our ability to love God and uncovering the divine at the center of all reality.

No Longer a Child

*God nurtures and caresses the soul, after it has been reso-
lutely converted to his service, like a loving mother. . . . But
as the child grows older, the mother withholds her caresses
and hides her tender love; . . . and sets the child down from
her arms, letting it walk on its own feet.* (*Dark Night* I.1.2)

Why not continue to pray in the same way we have prayed
for years, using images and reflection? Why rock the boat? After
all, this meditative form of prayer reinforced us emotionally and
inspired growth.

John's answer is simple: We come to a point in our spiritual
growth when we can no longer be held by our mother but need
to learn how to walk. Our relationship with God should not
be allowed to stagnate. In other words, as John explains in the
passage above, we are not meant to remain children who are
supported by the pleasure we receive from our prayer and the
control we have over our spiritual practice. Instead, we need to
grow up and walk, to learn how to mature in our love.

At the beginning of our prayer life, we are nurtured in the
ways of faith, hope, and love. Prayer is satisfying, and we think
we are making progress. We may even think we are more spir-
itually mature than others and perhaps look down on them.
Eventually, though, this comfortable world collapses. We are
tested, and we quickly realize that we are all too human, weaker
than we ever thought possible. Now we learn to pray again, but
in a dramatically different way: with a profound sense of our
dependence on God.

The journey from meditation, or reflective prayer, to contemplation, or silent and imageless prayer, inevitably involves sacrifice and the embrace of dryness and darkness. Coming to terms with the impenetrable night that we must travel through can be difficult for anyone who hears the call. The temptation stays with us: Why can't we simply remain in the warm, nurturing light?

However, John assures us that this is not the time to give up hope. We are simply outgrowing a childlike stage in the spiritual life and are in need of greater nourishment. We are awakening to the inner depths from a call that may have surfaced through friends, books, conversation, prayer, or a change in life circumstances—and responding. The experience of darkness challenges us to make a choice between growing in our desire for God, which leads to inexpressible mystery, or returning to spiritual experiences that we direct and that make us feel good about ourselves. No doubt we are influenced by our technological culture in this choice, because our culture emphasizes our ability to manipulate our lives and the world around us and is skeptical of knowledge that does not come from human enterprise and the senses.

The transition from meditation to contemplation may appear overwhelming, but two things should be remembered. First, John is not dictating a rigid program but is always aware that the Spirit works uniquely in each of our lives. Second, whatever our process, it depends entirely on grace; it is all gift. We become conscious of a loving presence in ourselves and in the world and realize it is entirely God's work. Our effort matters little. The only response is one of wonder and gratitude. The sheer giftedness of contemplation may be even more apparent to a person who has enjoyed this sense of divine nearness early in life without having thought much about it.

Generally, the transition from meditation to contemplation in most of our lives is a gentle progression, like a bud unfolding into a flower. Cultivating a love relationship with God through imagination and reflection eventually yields to the fullness, beauty, and silence of the blossoming rose. For John, this evolving prayer experience does not mean the end of meditative prayer—it may continue under the guidance of the Spirit—but the path of prayer is primarily contemplative, a graced call into the unknown.

A Love Story

They cannot actively purify themselves enough to be disposed in the least degree for the divine union of the perfection of love. God must take over. (Dark Night I.3.3)

Let's take a closer look at the transition from meditation to contemplation by using the analogy of a love relationship. One of the most appealing things about John is his willingness to talk about human love as a reflection of divine love.

At the beginning of our prayer life, we fall in love with God, a feeling that can last for a long time. This is the time of infatuation, when we depend upon our emotional involvement to help strengthen our relationship with God. As in any new relationship, we concentrate on an exchange, a give-and-take, with divine love, and talk intimately with God as to a friend. We also nurture a close friendship with the risen Jesus, who walks with us as he did with his disciples.

Our prayer life at this stage is active and includes a variety of forms that appeal to us. We ponder Scripture passages and faith mysteries, attend the liturgy, and do good works. Sometimes prayer at this stage takes the form of a spontaneous crying out to God during the day or the repetition of a mantra. At times this active prayer can draw us into a restful silence, where we experience a taste of contemplation, but this taste is still a result of our own effort that is helped by grace.

John does not spend much time with active prayer because he assumes that his reader has experienced it. While this assumption was appropriate for sixteenth-century Spain, when a faith relationship with the divine was considered the norm, in our secular culture, many are less interested in the faith dimension of life and less familiar with the prayer experience. It is more of a struggle for us to fit prayer of any kind into our daily lives.

Prayer that involves thoughts and images and feeds off our own effort can take us only so far on the journey to God. Human thoughts, no matter how inspiring, or human efforts, no matter how productive, are unable to prepare us for full union with divine love. Through contemplation, however, we are drawn into restful solitude and silence, and we depend less on thoughts and words. Each of us, according to John, has the potential to receive the gift of contemplation, yet few open themselves to it.

Because of the strong sense of God's love and nearness that is experienced in meditative prayer, we find ourselves led by faith into an unknown horizon, into a dark night. We develop a taste for a spiritual reality that is foreign to the senses. However, it is important to point out that John never abandons the senses for the sake of spiritual growth. Rather, he teaches that the senses are good in themselves and need to be integrated into the spiritual journey. Even so, through its participation in divine love, the soul eventually will develop a new way of seeing, loving, thinking, and acting, a way that originates in the Spirit and is foreign to the senses. Just as a human relationship is initially fed by enthusiasm and good feelings but over time settles into a deeper place of trust, commitment, inner peace, and shared silence, so too our relationship with God grows beyond the initial stages of prayer, and we wake up to a love relationship that feeds the depths of the soul in hidden ways.

The significant change that takes place between our initial way of praying and contemplation is that the former is active, mostly our doing, whereas the latter is passive, experienced as pure gift. Teresa of Ávila, using the metaphor of watering a garden, distinguishes between the labor of drawing the water by bucket and carrying it to the garden and the passivity of letting the garden be fed by the nurturing rain of divine love. The former is active and laborious, reaping the reward of good feelings and self-satisfaction; the latter is passive. However, "passive" doesn't mean that we do not participate but rather that our participation is receptive, that is, a response to the Spirit's work in us and no longer dictated by our own wishes.

John insists that human effort must give way eventually to divine activity; meditation must unfold into contemplation. It is God who leads us into the night of contemplation and prepares us to receive divine love on its own terms—the terms of grace, not merit. Darkness in this passive night heals the roots of harmful attachments and selfish preoccupations so that we can live out of a growing delight in the inner world. However, the temptation is to carry over our work ethic to contemplation, which is easy to do, particularly because this attitude is fostered in our practical, goal-oriented society. "Try a little harder," says the cultural voice, "and you can master anything." We are driven by past successes and find it difficult to release our grip on a project. John warns, however, that at this point on the spiritual journey, many without guidance falter and unintentionally subvert the hidden work of the Spirit.

According to John, once we have endured this stage of contemplation, which he refers to as the "passive night of sense," the inner tension releases itself and we experience a long interim of peace and inner tranquility. In other words, we have time to settle more deeply into a contemplative life and explore it. Eventually, though, rumblings in the unconscious get our attention, the inner struggle returns, and God invites a chosen few to experience the "passive night of the spirit." The sufferings experienced at this stage far exceed anything that went before and are outlined in the second book of *The Dark Night*. John tells us that this night completes the journey into darkness by "pulling up [the] roots" (*Dark Night* II.2.1) of our remaining imperfections.

Loving Attention

They must be content simply with a loving and peaceful attentiveness to God, and live without the concern, without the effort, and without the desire to taste or feel him. (*Dark Night* I.10.4)

Though John does not offer a method for contemplative prayer, he does offer guidance. He suggests that at some point, the use of thoughts and images in prayer becomes less and less fulfilling because we have received all that we can from this form of prayer. This is to be expected because all along, our prayer life has been drawing us toward a more simple relationship with God.

At some point, we become satisfied with a deeper and more peaceful love that requires few words, like an older couple walking silently hand in hand, simply enjoying each other's presence. This juncture is critical because for John, it contains all that is necessary for future growth in our spiritual life; it is like a seed that provides nourishment for everything that the plant needs. Sadly, many underestimate the importance of this transition or find it too difficult because they receive little support. If we find the strength to let go of images and thoughts and withdraw our effort, and if we are calm, we will be drawn into a deep silence and will eventually become aware of the presence of a "general loving knowledge of God" (*Ascent* II.13.7).

The example I find most helpful here is Brother Lawrence, a seventeenth-century Discalced friar who lived in Paris. Beyond practicing the usual recitation of prayers and devotional rituals,

Brother Lawrence found himself drawn by a desire to remain in the presence of God at all times. He found complex methods of prayer a barrier and insisted that we only need to create space throughout the day so that God can be present to us. His writings were gathered together after his death into a small collection called *The Practice of the Presence of God*. Here is Brother Lawrence's description of his prayer experience:

> I keep myself in His presence by simple attentiveness and a loving gaze upon God which I can call the actual presence of God. . . . As for time formally set aside for prayer, it is only a continuation of this same exercise. Sometimes I think of myself as a block of stone before a sculptor . . . and I beg Him to form His perfect image in my soul and make me entirely like Himself.[17]

If we make it a habit to bring ourselves into God's presence, an inner flame will come alive, and we will find ourselves living out of this loving awareness of God. This sense of divine presence, though difficult to perceive at first, will eventually become strong enough to remain with us all the time, even during our daily activities of cooking, cleaning, working at the computer, entertaining, or reading. A small flame awakens within us as divine energy and eventually evolves into a living flame of love, captivating our entire being and influencing all our actions and relationships.

Tourists who visit the Academia in Florence focus their attention primarily on the massive, ideal form of Michelangelo's sculptural masterpiece *David*. However, near the entrance of the museum stand his less conspicuous creations, called the *Slaves*, which are unfinished, partly sculpted figures that look as if they are struggling to break free of the stone. Michelangelo believed, as did Brother Lawrence, that our original form—the self in God—already exists and needs to be released. We, too, can imagine that we bear, in our heart of hearts, the image of Christ waiting to take form as beauty, simplicity, and poverty.

However, as John reminds us, we will be invited at some point in our lives to let go of our control and surrender our hammer and chisel into the creative hand of a divine Artist. We do this filled with hope, because forgoing our own efforts, we gain the unlimited creativity of a divine Sculptor who loves and forms us into the persons we were meant to be.

THE CHALLENGE OF DRY PRAYER

It is noteworthy that, however elevated God's communications and the experiences of his presence are, and however sublime a person's knowledge of him may be, these are not God essentially, nor are these comparable to him because, indeed, he is still hidden to the soul. Hence, regardless of all these lofty experiences, a person should think of him as hidden and seek him as one who is hidden, saying: "Where have You hidden?" (Canticle 1.3)

As I was reading Fr. Henri Nouwen's journal, *Sabbatical Journey,* written in the final year of his life, I came across a passage in which Henri admits that his prayer has dried up and that he no longer feels anything. He speculates that this darkness and dryness may be the result of increasing activity and less time in prayer but quickly realizes that this interpretation does not ring true.

Recalling Jesus' own sense of abandonment by God at the end of his life—a crisis that nevertheless led to new life—Henri wonders if his own experience of darkness and dryness could be a sign of a divine presence beyond anything he can think, sense, or imagine. Identifying with Jesus' dying, he realizes that "maybe the time has come to let go of *my* prayer, *my* effort to be close to God, *my* way of being in communion with the Divine, and allow the Spirit of God to blow freely in me."[18]

Henri's personal revelation rings true for many who are coping with dryness in prayer. He intuits that this dark contemplation is not a threat but a mysterious home for divine love, deeper than the human intellect, deeper than reason, feeling, and imagination. The challenge is to step aside, to practice a poverty of spirit or a willingness, as he puts it, to let go of *my* way of drawing close to God and give the Spirit room to work.

The dryness we experience in this transition from meditation to contemplation can present significant challenges. We are not accustomed to prayer that gives little or no pleasure but instead buries us in a midnight darkness, in an experience of desolation and dryness of soul and a sense of the absence of God. This prayer also heightens awareness of ourselves as finite creatures in need of God and intensifies the pain of our sinfulness. We are weaker than we ever imagined and truly dependent on divine mercy and love. No longer able to forge ahead under our own steam, we enter a spiritual desert. It is as if prayer itself has become painful and we can only bear it for a short time. We want to know when it all will end.

Even more troubling is the potential for this dryness to affect other areas of our life. For example, we find that we have little to give to others at home or at work, and the satisfaction we normally receive from our ministry disappears. I have heard dedicated ministers blaming others or their work for a loss of enthusiasm and a lack of patience. In some cases they need only to look inward and see that they are undergoing a profound change; their impasse was in fact a door opening.

A question remains: How can we tell whether our dryness and loss of desire is due to apathy toward prayer and the spiritual path or a process of the spirit being refined by God? Here are the signs that John gives that can help us decide whether we are involved in what he calls "the passive night of the senses":

- First, we experience no feeling of satisfaction in any area of our life, including prayer.

- Second, we try to maintain a spiritual life focused on serving God, but we seem to be spinning our wheels, and we no longer feel the immediacy of God's presence but only distance.

- Finally, the meditative prayer we are familiar with no longer appeals to us, and we find ourselves recognizing that prayer must come from a deeper Source and not from methods and spiritual practices that we choose. We feel drawn to do nothing but rest in the divine presence (*Ascent* II.13).

Perhaps the greatest challenge in a time of dryness is that we have to trust that love exists deeper than feeling and that the best prayer may be the prayer in which nothing seems to be happening. We have grown accustomed to looking for special experiences or signs to indicate spiritual growth; now we are called in contemplation to simply rest in a loving presence without expectation. John summarizes it this way: "All that is required of them here is freedom of soul, that they liberate themselves from the impediment and fatigue of ideas and thoughts, and care not about thinking and meditating. They must be content simply with a loving and peaceful attentiveness to God, and live without the concern, without the effort, and without the desire to taste or feel him" (*Dark Night* 10.4). John calls us to a deepening faith, one that we could never have imagined.

Finally, it is important to note that John favors desert dryness at every stage of spiritual growth because he believes that it forms us into the person we should become. Dryness empties us of a false reliance on self and deepens our awareness of our humble dependency on Someone beyond us. The cross, then, is the ultimate reason to embrace dryness, according to John, because Jesus passed through a night of abandonment on the way to the resurrection.

Growing in Self-Knowledge

The first and chief benefit this dry and dark night of contemplation causes is the knowledge of self and of one's own misery. (Dark Night I.12.2)

Perhaps the greatest fear that arises with contemplation is that I will lose myself. Who will I be if I allow myself to surrender completely to divine love?

In meditative prayer, we were able to retain a strong image of self because the emotional payoff that comes with this form of prayer reinforces the self-image we project. We feel good because we receive signs from God that we are growing. In the dryness of contemplative prayer, however, our emotions are not reinforced. Rather, the old self-image becomes porous, revealing the light of an inner truth, namely, my identity in the love and mercy of God. At this point, the question is "Who am I?"

In addition, at an earlier stage of our inner journey, we redirected harmful desires and created an environment for further spiritual growth. We felt good about our efforts. However, now we realize that we have only scratched the surface because the deep roots of those desires are exposed and further work on our part is useless. We have to hand over our lives completely to God in a passive night.

At this point, we are tempted to return to a more familiar, predictable path or even stop praying. A great deal is at stake with contemplation because we are involved in a dramatically different relationship with God. We can no longer hold on to the old self because this image now reveals itself as illusory and inauthentic, based on the expectations of others and on our own egocentrism; nor can we simply introduce another more suitable image. God will not have a relationship with an illusion we create but only with an authentic person.

However, if we open ourselves to the hidden light of contemplation, it will continue to expose the secret rooms of the heart, one after another, healing interior wounds and awakening sorrow for past sins. This light strengthens our determination to change and nurtures a healthy inner climate for love. John does not ask us to concentrate on our sinfulness but rather to keep our gaze on the light, allowing its radiance to guide us toward deeper self-knowledge and humility. For example, when we are wiping haze from a foggy window, we do not focus on the haze but on the scene the clear window will reveal. Awareness of our sinfulness, then, should not take our attention away from the inner light of love.

With the self-knowledge that comes through contemplation, we see ourselves as we truly are: completely dependent on divine love and mercy. Humility, after all, is simply knowledge of self in the light of divine truth. Our response is to have faith in the darkness that enfolds us and embrace the mystery of the cross. For the first time, from the depths of our being, we can say, "Lord, have mercy," and truly mean it. We have to ask for the forgiveness of our sins only once, not continually. Instead, we trust in divine mercy, the steadfast love of God, to remain with us and give us strength.

Self-knowledge, for John, means choosing the cross. Our decision to embrace the cross in our daily lives entails a willingness to stand before God in all our poverty and nakedness, with no interest in returning to our old self-image. We choose to live with our limitations and to accept our humanness. This humble posture of heart reveals a self completely dependent on God and connected to a shared humanity; this sense of communion can never be explained but only experienced.

Who am I? What is my authentic self? I am loved, I am precious in God's eyes, and I am a sinner for whom Christ died. I do not love God in order to get something back; loving and seeking God is its own reward. This knowledge is reinforced continually in contemplation.

THE NEED FOR SPIRITUAL GUIDANCE

If there is no one to understand these persons, they either turn back and abandon the road or lose courage. (Dark Night I.10.2)

At this stage on the spiritual path, it is clear that unless we receive guidance or reinforcement from books, counseling, trusted friends, or another source, we will falter. We need support—John is adamant on this point.

For John, the movement from meditation to contemplation is a critical and necessary juncture in the spiritual path, not because we are choosing a new way of praying, but because our lives are being reshaped dramatically. Do we continue to put our own desires first and look for personal satisfaction in our spiritual growth, or do we offer ourselves completely to divine love? An answer is emerging from the depths of one's being; however, the pull to return to the familiar, well-trodden path is strong. Without spiritual reinforcement, it is easy to falter or even turn back.

In his time, John was upset with spiritual guides who did not encourage growth toward a deeper intimacy with God. His own guidance always took into consideration the uniqueness of a person's journey and the primacy of the Spirit's work in a person's life. Today many hunger for information and support but find few resources. This can certainly be expected since the desert experience that is essential to contemplation runs directly contrary to our cultural and even religious expectations today. We are practical, consumer-oriented people focused on accumulating goods and experiences, not on simplicity and sacrifice for the sake of spiritual growth.

I recently met a middle-aged woman who told me she was unable to pray because she could no longer feel God's presence. Her love for God was palpable in the tone of her voice, but she was frustrated because her prayer had dried up, and she felt that she had been abandoned at a time of profound need. As we talked, others entered the conversation, and soon everyone was encouraging her to see the darkness as a time of fertile growth. God was not absent, they reassured her, but only hidden. I walked away from the exchange in wonder at the spiritual wisdom that surfaced at a critical time. I was encouraged that the Spirit works in subtle ways to guide us and that those who trust their journey will find a surprising number of people who can relate to them from their own experience.

John acknowledges that the process of letting go of control without guidance can be difficult but encourages us not to lose courage; we should continue to believe that our hand is being held even in the dark, dry times. He warns that many "fatigue and overwork themselves, thinking that they are failing because of their negligence or sins," when in fact, "Those who are in this situation should feel comforted; they ought to persevere patiently and not be afflicted. Let them trust in God who does not fail those who seek him with a simple and righteous heart" (*Dark Night* I.10.2, 3).

John himself demonstrated empathy as a spiritual guide. He did not map out the journey and then leave a person to fend for himself. In a letter that reveals him to be a gentle and wise guide, he offers consolation to a woman who feels that God has abandoned her:

> While you are in darkness and emptiness of spiritual poverty, you think that everyone and everything are failing you. This is not surprising, for then it also seems to you that God is failing you too. But nothing is wanting to you. . . . You are in a good way. Be quiet and rejoice.[19]

In the end, however, John considered the Holy Spirit to be the most important spiritual guide. A good spiritual director or retreat leader considers herself a conduit for the Spirit's work. In *The Living Flame of Love*, he makes it clear that "the whole concern of directors should not be to accommodate souls to their own method and condition, but they should observe the road along which God is leading one; if they do not recognize it, they should leave the soul alone and not bother it" (*Flame* 3.46).

What would John emphasize in spiritual direction today? For someone who wants to move beyond the emotional rewards of a charismatic spirituality or who is at a point in life when the simplicity of the desert becomes attractive, I suspect that he would encourage contemplative prayer, which is an ongoing transformation that leads through darkness to a deeper trust in infinite love. His path involves daily attention to sacrifice of any habits, desires, thoughts, and behavior that might restrict the heart's openness to continued growth in faith and love.

Let us now explore this darkness, this journey in which we recognize that nothing can satisfy our deepest needs but God alone.

Suggestions for Reflection

1. Practice a gentle, loving awareness of God as you go through your daily life. Turn aside for a moment or two from your activity and direct your attention to God. Believe, as John suggests, that this simple practice will ignite a flame in your soul.

2. Set aside twenty minutes or more every day for centering prayer. Sit or lie down in a comfortable position with your back straight and your body at ease. Take two or three deep breaths, inhaling and exhaling slowly and deliberately. Realize that for the next twenty minutes, you will do nothing, produce nothing, and communicate nothing. Your intention is simply to remain open to the divine presence.

   Your intention is primary. However, you can intend to be open to God and find that in a short time, your mind has begun to roam and you are thinking of plans for tomorrow. Determine that each time you get distracted, you will let the thought go and begin again without getting down on yourself. The idea is not to get somewhere but to return again and again to the center, to an open receptivity; each return is an act of love because it is a choice to empty the self for God.

Select a simple word that appeals to you as prayerful— a word like "Jesus," "Lord," "Father," "Word," "Spirit," "Light," "Bread," "Truth," or "Beloved." If you feel yourself slipping out of prayer and into distraction, repeat the word gently. Repeat your prayer word to yourself as a means of letting go of the thought that has caught your attention. However, you do not have to repeat the word constantly; it acts as a guide back to the center. Then be still again. At the close of centering time, slowly pray the Our Father as a transition from passivity to active involvement.

3. Remember that contemplative prayer is not limited to words or even silence; it can flow from and through everything we do. God's creative impulse to express something of the divine in creation also finds expression in our own creativity. What gifts are entrusted to you? Let your response to your gifts become your prayer; let your work express what is in your heart.

CHAPTER FIVE

WALKING IN DARKNESS

O guiding night!
O night more lovely than the dawn!
—*The Dark Night*, stanza 5

Several years ago, during a period of mental and physical exhaustion, I went on a retreat to regain a sense of balance in my life. I thought I simply needed rest and time to reflect. But after a few days, it became apparent that the exhaustion had hidden a deeper spiritual weariness: I had lost inner peace and a feeling of gratitude for my life. Everything I had once depended on—inner tranquility, attraction to prayer, and a sense of God's nearness—had abandoned me. The long-standing sense of divine presence was gone; I was lost and uncertain. It is difficult to describe how deeply disoriented I was; I only knew that my usual supports had been stripped away, and I was questioning everything. Was my faith an illusion? Was it only an expression of my ego? What kind of God did I believe in?

During a long walk, I tried to find pleasure in the natural beauty of the forest path, but the landscape seemed dull and distant. When I turned inward and tried to rest prayerfully, God seemed absent, and I felt estranged from myself. Only one intuition kept reoccurring: Surrender to the darkness. This is the word that I carried in my heart, and it gave me some peace.

After several days it felt as if a heavy cloak were being lifted from my shoulders, and something new began to emerge within me. The restlessness was not as strong, and I was able to find pleasure in the beauty around me, especially the simple enjoyment of the sun's warmth, the play of light and shadow, and the rhythm of day and night. I remember rising at dawn with a sense that the sunlight was filling every cell of my being. I seemed resurrected and transformed both inside and out. Nothing dramatic occurred; everything was familiar but somehow different in my eyes.

A simple awareness gleaned from this inner renewal stayed with me long after I returned home: gratitude. I was thankful for my very being and for the world around me. Small events caught my attention: the rhythm of my breath, a butterfly in a field, a branch of leaves shuddering in a breeze. Thankfulness cascaded from one moment to another. Life itself took form as an ongoing prayer of gratitude.

Some time later, while rereading John's description of the dark night, I realized that my experience sounded familiar. For John, the darkness is a path toward union that is hidden in mystery. We discover an invitation to a deeper faith, one that invites a person to trust a God beyond words, images, symbols, and the usual feelings. All of this is a challenge, and we question whether or not all has been lost. As John writes, "If the soul in traveling this road leans on any elements of its own knowledge or of its experience or knowledge of God, it will easily go astray or be detained because it did not desire to abide in complete blindness, in the faith that is its guide" (*Ascent* II.4.3).

At the time, though my usual sense of reality was undercut, I found comfort in the insight that God dwells in darkness beyond images, imagination, and reasoning, and that none of these could fully express the divine. The very idea of depending less on familiar spiritual props and resting in the darkness brought enormous relief, as if my heart had found a home. I was surprised that it was possible to choose the darkness as a path, though it meant the loss of habitual ways of seeing that I had once treasured.

Introduction to a Dark Path

The soul must ordinarily walk this path (dark night) to reach that sublime and joyous union with God. (Dark Night, Prologue)

It is easy to presume that John's description of the dark night applies mostly to members of a contemplative community or to those few in secular life who have enough time for solitude and silence. In fact, he believed that the darkness is an ordinary path experienced by all who take their spiritual lives seriously, practice their faith, and lead a life grounded in virtue. He also considered the dark night to be an aspect of the spiritual journey that we might experience more than once, because we are always learning what it means to allow divine love to draw close.

John of the Cross experienced his own dark night of the soul when his captors threw him into a tiny cell. Here is an interpretation from one of his biographers:

He suffered the complete absence of God. It was not just a light, momentary absence, such as most believers know from experience. It was total. All his life, past and present, seemed to him to be wasted. He could no longer pray. The very thought of God made him sick, even physically sick. He felt abandoned in his degradation.[20]

Although John's ordeal was dramatic, it is an experience that to some degree each of us may encounter. For example, it can be triggered in any number of ways in the course of our own lives: a death in the family, a job loss, a cancer diagnosis, failed dreams, or stress from busyness. Theologian Belden Lane, who writes on the desert experience, reveals that his own journey into the unknown began when he accompanied his mother on her journey through cancer, from her diagnosis to the experience of a nursing home to her eventual death. He admits, "Certain truths can be learned, it seems, only as one is sufficiently emptied, frightened, or confused."[21]

There are also transition times that all of us undergo, like middle age, when we feel an imperative to turn our attention away from preoccupations outside of ourselves and move inward. We realize that we no longer want to meet the expectations of others or behave in response to social conditioning; comfortable masks no longer afford protection. We find ourselves walking a dark path with the invitation to trust God in naked faith.

The human experience of God at these times is darkness, primarily because the divine work of transforming our lives remains hidden. According to psychiatrist Gerald May, "The dark night of the soul is not an event one passes through and gets beyond, but rather a deep ongoing process that characterizes our spiritual life. In this sense, the dark night *is* a person's hidden life with God."[22]

Our first response to the discovery of this dark river of meaning that is flowing through our lives is to interpret it and try to regulate it. But after failed attempts, we wonder where God is and why God is not helping us. Divine love seems to desert us in prayer and in our daily lives, and we are left in dryness and darkness.

John advises that we persevere in the darkness and trust that God is near. In other words, we should immerse ourselves in its mysterious depths and rest there, letting faith center us. Eventually, our vision will change; faith will mature, and we will discover that all along, we have been walking this path. It was only our limitations that prevented us from seeing with new eyes and enjoying a sense of divine presence. For John, there is a dramatic difference between our experience of God and who God is in himself. God is darkness to us but light in himself.

WALKING AN UNKNOWN ROAD

To reach a new and unknown land and travel unknown roads, a man cannot be guided by his own knowledge. . . . The soul, too, when it advances, walks in darkness and unknowing. (Dark Night II.16.8)

At the beginning of the spiritual journey, we enter into darkness by letting go of harmful attachments and selfish preoccupations to live a life of virtue. This redirection of our desires toward God alone is an active night; while we rely on grace, it invites our full participation. At this stage we are pilgrims starting a new adventure, feeling the joy of God's presence in prayer and developing a friendship with Jesus.

Later, as John puts it, the darkness is no longer dusk but midnight darkness. This is a time when we learn to depend fully on the gift of grace, the inflow of a loving God. Though we participate, this darkness is primarily God's work in us; our participation is mostly receptive.

Our journey into the night is a journey of deepening faith. It leads us through an inner desert on a path to union with Christ. We follow the glimmer of a star, the true self in Christ, which appears as a momentary flash of radiance but most often remains hidden behind clouds. The desert experience plays an important role in Carmelite tradition, beginning with the small group of hermits who settled around the spring of Elijah to lead a life of contemplative solitude and silence. Without the desert times in our lives, we gain little self-knowledge, and our desire for God weakens. In the desert we set aside our own agenda and embrace a more mature faith. The desert darkness itself gives us the opportunity to discover whether we are serious about our desire for God or whether this is only one concern among many.

What does the night journey into the unknown feel like? It feels like the Sinai experience of the Israelites or the journey of the Magi. These desert travelers learned to rely on God rather than themselves, to trust in something greater and persevere in the darkness. In the wild, God has our attention and takes us by the hand, testing us each step of the way. Do we want to depend on our own resources or on divine love? With each faltering step, we realize how in need we are in our vulnerability and sinfulness.

One example of a desert experience that may offer some guidance for a community today is that of the Jewish people. Although they longed for peace and fulfillment, just as we do, they had to find the mystery of God in chaos and darkness. Forced to leave behind their temple, the center of their worship, they retained the memory of their history, rituals, and family relationships, all of which helped them as they tried to make a home in a foreign land. Most of all, they preserved their faith, and in time, their faith moved inward. The prophet Jeremiah predicted this turn inward: "Look, the days are coming, Yahweh declares, when I shall make a new covenant with the house of Israel (and the House of Judah). . . . Within them I shall plant my Law, writing it on their hearts. Then I shall be their God and they will be my people" (31:31, 33).

The sacred rolls of the Torah may have been destroyed when the Temple was razed, but those in the covenant community uncovered the law of God written in their hearts, and this became the foundation of their life together. The exile experience taught them to trust in a hidden God in a time of suffering and disorientation. Many today can identify with these exiles because they find themselves disenchanted by cultural promises and feel drawn to an ineffable darkness and a desert God.

Once you travel into the unknown without the usual supports, with only faith as your guide, the experience will have far-reaching effects. In T. S. Eliot's poem "Journey of the Magi," one of the Magi recounts his trials and tribulations in the desert and wonders what the journey was all about. He had experienced birth, but the birth was difficult, like death. He surmises that the experiences of birth and death are somehow linked. One thing is certain, he acknowledges: He will never be comfortable with the old ways, with the palaces and the opulence. But it doesn't matter, since he has discovered a new life.

Where Is God?

God is also a dark night to the soul in this life. (*Ascent* I.2.1)

One of the great trials of the dark night is our sense that God is absent and that we have been abandoned. We feel the weight of God's hand on us but cannot see it. There is no sense of divine presence in prayer, and we are tempted to think that we have done something wrong, that God's absence is our own fault. This guilt can be overwhelming, but it is not warranted. John assures us that God is not absent but hiding; divine presence is veiled.

As beginners on the path, we project an image of God that is based on our own needs. God is "out there," removed from us but ready to help us when called upon. This image may provide strength and joy and further our growth by helping us move beyond harmful attachments. Also, on rare occasions we may even catch a glimpse of divine love powerful enough to awaken our souls and give us the inspiration to forge ahead.

As the night deepens, however, not only do we lose our usual sense of being in control, which we experience as desert dryness, but we also find that our former image of God disappears. We are left only with painful darkness, the distance between self and God. We no longer have easy access to God and the pleasure that this once brought us: "God darkens all this light and closes the door and the spring of sweet spiritual water they were tasting as often and as long as they desired" (*Dark Night* I.8.3). In other words, we find ourselves in a wilderness seemingly without resources of thought, feeling, or imagination, and we think we are abandoned.

Perhaps we now appreciate how much our former perception of God was an exercise of the intellect and the imagination, one that reflected more of us than of God. Freed from an image that is strongly linked to our own frame of reference, we discover a God totally other than ourselves, the Holy revealed as ineffable.

This experience of an incomprehensible God cannot be underestimated. It is so difficult because suddenly we lack moorings and seem to be drifting without a rudder. The first inclination is to retrieve our former way of relating to God and the spiritual practices that accompanied it. Retreating, however, will undermine the very heart of our journey. John warns that "in searching for spirit, they lose the spirit that was the source of their tranquility and peace" (*Dark Night* I.10.1).

It would seem that this experience of distance would be the last thing we would desire because of the pain and darkness it involves. However, as John asserts, love drives us increasingly to a higher form of divine love; it will not settle for anything but union.

Today, many understand how easy it is to settle for a cozy image of God that fulfills our emotional needs and provides a quick and easy way to live our faith. They yearn for a relationship with God that does not fulfill them as much as tests them. They want a wilderness God who is not limited to their intellect and imagination. As theologian Belden Lane writes, "God disguises himself, hiding in a manger, his majesty veiled upon a cross, so that we might irresistibly be drawn to a grace far closer than we ever imagined."[23] John speaks to all those today who ache for the mystery that can only be found by wandering in a trackless desert. However, it is a desert in which we are not alone but guided by a hidden love more intimate to us than we can imagine.

Finally, for those who find it difficult to move beyond an image of a powerful, judging God who controls their lives, it is helpful to imagine that the divine is playfully hiding so that we learn to seek, feigning absence so that we can mature in love. For John, our relationship with God is primarily a relationship between the lover and the Beloved, and so it can seem like foolishness to an onlooker. Reading his poems, especially *The Dark Night* and *The Spiritual Canticle*, we find ourselves pulled in by God's playfulness, engaged in a divine game of hide-and-seek. For example, in *The Spiritual Canticle*, the seeker asks with a heavy heart, "Where have you hidden, / Beloved, and left me moaning?" (stanza 1).

The Pain of the Dark Night

There is nothing in contemplation or the divine inflow that of itself can give pain; contemplation rather bestows sweetness and delight. . . . The cause for not experiencing these agreeable effects is the soul's weakness and imperfection. (*Dark Night* II.9.11)

The dark night is God's work, but God does not cause the pain. John assures us that the pain of the dark night comes not from God's presence, the inflow of love, but from the all too human resistance to this love. Because of human imperfection, we are not empty enough for the fullness of God's presence, and furthermore, we are too distracted by our many preoccupations to pay attention to our plight. As a result, we experience undue anguish and torment (*Dark Night* II.5.1–2).

The pain can be intense because God, a divine Artist working the clay of our being, hollows out places within us that we never knew existed, opening the secret caverns of the heart in need of healing. The roots of our faults and imperfections are mostly hidden, and only in the receptivity of this night can they be exposed and removed. What about the deep roots of our fears— the anxieties in our personal unconscious—and even deeper, the archetypes that all humans share? Journeying through this mysterious darkness only intensifies this process of purification and healing.

Who will accept the consequences of putting his life into the hands of a divine Artist and allowing it to be reformed?

At one point, I was curious about the potter's craft and wanted to learn how to "throw" a small bowl. "Throwing" is a technique for centering a lump of clay on a circulating wheel and forming it. I asked a friend to teach me. She demonstrated the process of kneading a handful of clay, a technique that would ensure an even consistency in the clay ball, allowing it to be more easily thrown on the wheel.

Holding the lump of clay in my hand, I remember thinking, "This is me; *this* is my life. Do I really want to hand it over completely and have it molded by God's loving touch? How am I going to resolve this tension I feel?"

Imagine that the divine Artist begins to form us by gently pressing thumb and fingers into the middle of a revolving mound of clay. Using an image that fits well with the making of pottery,

John writes that "the hand of God does not press down or weigh on the soul, but only touches it; and this mercifully, for God's aim is to grant it favors and not to chastise it" (*Dark Night* II.5.7). The clay responds in turn, releasing itself little by little to the pressure. Walls begin to rise, at first thick and heavy, weighed down by self-interest, but eventually thinner and more lyrical, making room for the activity of love.

We wonder how we will find the courage and strength to respond to the Potter's touch and allow the walls of our being to swell upward into a thin and delicate form.

Being squeezed, stretched, and extended is painful because we have settled for a stagnant life with no form. Losing this old self as the clay thins and spirals upward escalates fear of the unknown and can drive us back into familiar patterns of behavior, practices, and ways of praying. Trust falters. Who finds surrender easy, even surrender that promises boundless love? Yet through the pain of the experience, we uncover a secret: If we stay in sync with an inner music—the rhythm of the Spirit—we feel free and more at peace with the process of growth.

In the end, we understand that hope lies not in our effort as clay to create our lives but on the creativity and energy of the Artist. As we accept this important truth, the journey gains its own momentum. Love does not draw us toward an ideal of perfection but toward surrender; it is not about our goals but about remaining moist and supple so that we can be stretched by the dynamism of love.

John assures us that God wants an intimate relationship with us, but as we draw close, divine love simultaneously stretches and transforms us. The Holy Spirit teaches us what we need to know through the inflow of divine love. John writes, "God teaches the soul secretly and instructs it in the perfection of love without its doing anything or understanding how this happens" (*Dark Night* II.5.1). His favorite image, one popular with medieval mystics, is the log of wood. When it is first lit, a log smokes, hiding the flame, but gradually the wood is transformed and becomes bright and glowing (*Dark Night* II.10). The soul with its many imperfections undergoes a process of cleansing by the fire of divine love until it becomes a flame.

In the end, pain is not the final word. Suffering itself enlarges our capacity to bear pain, but it also enlarges our capacity for joy. Why? "The purest suffering brings with it the purest and most intimate knowing, and consequently the purest and highest joy, because it is a knowing from further within" (*Canticle* 36.12).

CRIES IN THE NIGHT

Because it seems that God has rejected it, the soul suffers such pain and grief that when God tried Job in this way it proved one of the worst of Job's trials. (Dark Night II.5.5)

We have seen how praying in the darkness can be unbearable. We feel as if we have lost God, and the pain of this loss leaves us in a state of depression and confusion. We wonder what went wrong. Where is my relationship with the divine, my prayer?

The figure of Job gives us an example of a prayer that rises out of a sense of isolation and seeming absence of the divine. Job's prayer is a cry from the depths, deeper than the self, the cry of the Spirit within us who knows our pain.

Job teaches a prayer to those who experience the loss of power on every level—the disenfranchised, the poor, and those suffering from injustice. John's own prayer arose from his sense of powerlessness. He was imprisoned because his prophetic presence challenged others, even though he was simply responding to his call. His prayer, like Job's, arose from the darkness of faith being tested. His heart, like Job's, cried out from the depths. It was the voice of faith discovering a prayer deeper than words, arising like a storm from the unconscious.

Jesus discovered his own night prayer at Gethsemane: "But this is your hour; this is the reign of darkness" (Luke 22:53). Gethsemane was the center of inner struggle and turmoil. Prostrating himself on the ground, Jesus cries out, "My Father, . . . if it is possible, let this cup pass me by. Nevertheless, let it be as you, not I, would have it" (Matthew 26:39). He pleads with his disciples, as tired as they are, not to fall asleep. There is urgency in his voice because, as he tells the disciples, remaining awake will not only support him but obtain their own salvation. The door to eternal happiness opens for the disciples, but they must be ready to pass through it. Sadly, they fall asleep.

Jesus continues to pray from the center of his anguish, and eventually finds a deep peace. No longer overwhelmed by his ordeal, he discovers a new prayer and asserts with confidence that he will obey his Father's will: "Am I not to drink the cup that the Father has given me?" (John 18:11).

Night prayers are all born out of our struggle to trust in a will that we cannot know. Each of us will learn this prayer—perhaps at the bedside of a dying loved one. And with the gift of faith, we will discover that Gethsemane and the cross lead not to an overwhelming sense of abandonment but to a life of resurrected glory.

Suggestions for Reflection

1. When have you found your sense of control abandoning you? What prayer did your heart provide you in this darkness?

2. Interior confusion and anxiety, often initiated by suffering and loss, may threaten our very being, but as John of the Cross suggests, they may also help us face a difficult truth in our lives. When have your tears been the occasion for insight? What was this difficult truth that you encountered?

3. In what way do you feel the "touch" of the divine Artist molding your life? Review some of the activities and prayers in your daily life. Which of them seem to be the occasion for releasing self and expanding your heart?

Chapter Six

Trusting This Holy Darkness

O night that has united
the Lover with his beloved,
transforming the beloved in her Lover.
—*The Dark Night*, stanza 5

At the beginning of the story of Job, we are introduced to a good man who pays attention to religious ritual and worships a judging God. But through the experience of terrible suffering—the loss of all he holds dear—he is forced to encounter a God beyond his imagination and expectation. Discovering the Holy at the center of a whirlwind, he finds that the divine is not as accessible as he once thought, and he is humbled in the face of Mystery. "Where were you when I laid the earth's foundations?" God asks (Job 38:4).

Job admits that he has heard about God from others, but now he "sees" God face-to-face: "Before, I knew you only by hearsay but now, having seen you with my own eyes, I retract what I have said" (Job 42:5-6). His "seeing" is contemplation, an immediate intuitive awareness of a divine Presence who is wild and escapes definition. Job trusts this wilderness God because the darkness of his suffering has taught him that this is the very Mystery he has longed to encounter.

We, too, if we trust a wild God and accept the grace of the contemplative path, learn to live in the darkness and discover that God alone is sufficient. Our heart yearns for an ineffable stillness in the stillness beyond words. What we say becomes less important than listening to the word spoken in the depths of the heart. Even in the noise and busyness of daily life, we find the capacity to wait, listen, and be attentive. Faith deepens, and though at times we experience the darkest of nights, divine love never abandons us. All along, as Thomas Keating says, "God simply moves downstairs, so to speak, and waits for us to come and join him."[24]

In this final chapter, we will explore what it means to trust and grow in this fertile darkness. This is not a time of doing and thinking but of being and unknowing; we are challenged to enter a completely different relationship with God. The darkness is ongoing, a symbol of our entire journey; it has meant abandoning pleasure in worldly attachments, a night of the senses. It also entails following a path of faith that is darkness to the intellect. Finally, God's own self is darkness to us in this life. In the end, the dark path is a process of learning to disappear completely into an intimacy that we cannot touch and to belong fully to a light that we cannot see.

I once saw an inspiring documentary entitled "Gifts from the Fire," which describes the creative process of the late renowned ceramic artist Brother Thomas Bezanson. In the film Brother Thomas talks about a recurrent dream in which he envisions a white pot so simple and pure that it seems translucent. In the dream he is so captivated by the image that he tries to make the pot repeatedly, and each time he fails. Eventually, his energy gives out and the dream fades. Years later, during a trip to visit fellow potters in Japan, it occurs to him that the white pot might represent his deepest self, his desire to disappear into the light of truth and unity. The rightness of this intuition startles him, and he accepts this symbol as the goal of his life.

John of the Cross also insists that we allow ourselves to be taught by a transformative darkness so that our existence becomes pure light, and our identity, a blazing vessel. For John, the way of *nada* (nothing) is the way of night that leads to *todo* (all), the fullness of divine light. From the beginning it has been a journey of love and faith, leading into the deepest caverns of the heart that only love can transform.

John does not call us to some ideal perfection but to holiness, to a relationship with God in which union with the Beloved is all. Like the potter Brother Thomas, he dreams of the fullness of light: "When light shines on a clean and pure crystal [the soul], . . . it can become so brilliant from the abundance of light received that it seems to be all light" (*Flame* 1.13)

How, then, do we learn to engage this holy darkness so that it can teach us to become "all light"? Since this passive night is God's doing, the secret is to wait, trust, and have faith that the dawn is near. We live in hope of the light.

LEARNING TO WAIT PATIENTLY

They should allow the soul to remain in rest and quietude even though it may seem obvious to them that they are doing nothing and wasting time, and even though they think this disinclination to think about anything is due to their laxity. (Dark Night I.10.4)

In our pragmatic culture, the tendency is to figure things out and take control. If we experience a setback, we seek a quick resolution so that we can waylay suffering and get on with our lives. We are fixated on the quick and easy and become impatient with any kind of waiting.

In his autobiography, *Report to Greco*, Nikos Kazantzakis tells of a time when he was completely drained of energy and went to see a hermit on Mount Athos for counsel. The hermit told him to wait. Nikos became frustrated and wanted to know how long. The hermit replied, "Until salvation ripens in you. Allow time for the sour grape to turn to honey."[25] Nikos waited in a hermitage, not knowing what to expect, but nevertheless trusting. One day in winter, he looked out his window and saw a medlar tree blossoming. Tears of joy welled up in him because he knew immediately that his prayers had been answered.

Perhaps at some point in our lives, through the experience of a crisis brought on by exhaustion, a life transition, an illness, or a persistent inner voice, we may also have heard the invitation to wait, to step aside and trust that the waiting itself would bear fruit. It was a difficult choice, but we recognized that it was no longer primarily about our activity but about God's activity. We trusted that the Spirit was at work in our lives, creating space, healing inner wounds, and bringing us to wholeness, though we knew nothing about it. We were ready to accept that uncovering new life meant not restless searching but remaining still.

As John points out, waiting in the presence of divine love may seem like a waste of time, but we are actively participating in creating room for hidden work. By resting in God, we practice a passive receptivity, "content simply with a loving and peaceful attentiveness to God" (*Dark Night* I.10.4). John asks only that we let go of any tendency to use ideas or images or of any desire to feel a divine presence, because all these bind the soul and weigh it down, making it too tired and anxious to remain attentive.

He uses the example of a painter's model to describe what happens if we allow ourselves to be distracted as we wait (*Dark Night* I.10.5). If the model moves as the painter tries to capture the form on canvas, then the painting will have to be discarded. In the same way, if we are resting in silent prayer and allow ourselves to cling to a desire for some intellectual or emotional reinforcement, then our inner peace will be shattered and we will be left with a sense of emptiness. In effect, we chose something limited as a way of satisfying a desire for the unlimited.

Initially, it may be difficult to follow the counsel to wait, to just "be still, and know that I am God!" (Psalm 46:10, NRSV). But eventually trust in darkness ripens, and we find our entire being collected into a unified whole, like a ballet dancer on point. No longer do we hold on to some passing thought or image, but rather, we let go and sink completely into a loving presence. John counsels that at first we may not feel any longing for God, only dryness, making the darkness difficult to bear. But in time a flame will come alive, firing our deepest longing. It is this flame that anchors our waiting even in the midst of activity. In the end, we learn that waiting, learning "to be," is a condition of the soul and a simple gift.

After the crucifixion, a curtain of darkness closed around the disciples as they huddled in fear, panic, and isolation. How would they respond to Jesus' absence? He who was their source of strength, inspiration, and consolation, who walked alongside them daily, was no longer present in their midst. Did the disciples realize that this painful night, when all hope seemed to vanish and they were forced to wait, might be a time to explore a new form of relationship?

When Jesus, abandoned and uncertain, waited in the garden of Gethsemane, his suffering formed itself in these words: "My Father, . . . if it is possible, let this cup pass me by. Nevertheless, let it be as you, not I, would have it" (Matthew 26:39). Where was his Father? What would the night bring? Time was no longer his; he could only allow his heart to be emptied in obedience to his Father's will. Both Jesus and his disciples teach us that waiting patiently without recourse to distraction means suffering because we hand over our lives repeatedly and learn trust. It is trial by darkness and a sense of abandonment but also an opportunity for growth. In time, vulnerability is transformed into strength and trust deepens. The soul, now bone dry, becomes strong.

GUIDED INTO SOLITUDE

In this solitude, away from all things, the soul is alone with God and he guides, moves, and raises her to divine things. (Canticle 35. \5)

Throughout his life John hungered for quiet times to be alone with God. This deep love for silence and solitude eventually brought him to the door of the Carmelite Order. Even a busy schedule did not prevent him from finding time for solitude. During a stay in Lisbon, he went off alone, Bible in hand, and walked along the seashore, gazing at the expanse of the Atlantic, reading and meditating.

Just before the end of his life, John's opposition to some of the decisions of the new vicar general led to his exile at the isolated monastery in La Penuela in the region of Andalusia. Rather than rebelling at the rejection, he saw it as an opportunity to immerse himself in the welcomed silence of the place, and he would rise each morning before daybreak to say his morning prayer among a group of willow trees. Even when he was forced to leave the monastery due to a serious infection, he wrote to a friend, "I intend, however, to return here as quickly as possible, for it is certain that I am very well in this solitude."[26]

Many today understand the value of solitude and silence because there is a great need to find sanity in the midst of our frenetic world. According to John, though, we do not so much choose solitude and silence—as important as this is—but rather, solitude chooses us. The pull toward solitude arises out of the inner transformation of a contemplative. As soon as a soul is free to love, then God draws it into solitude. God wounds the heart in such a way that it sees everything in the light of divine love, and the world seems like "nothing." It is this light of divine love, the inner flame, which allows us to see all reality as it truly is: as completely dependent on God. This light of divine love *is* our solitude and silence.

In this solitude our personal preferences take a backseat, and God can be God in our lives. Because we truly love God, we get out of the way and let go of what we want God to be. In short, the soul finally discovers the capacity to listen deeply to its true voice. It remains purely receptive, aware of its giftedness.

The problem is that as soon as we revert back to the comfort and security of our old ways and give in to distractions, solitude disappears, and that secret inner space within us collapses under the weight of our noisy thoughts and insistent desires. John of the Cross emphasizes that "it is impossible for this highest wisdom and language of God, which is contemplation, to be received in anything less than a spirit that is silent and detached from discursive knowledge and gratification" (*Flame* 3.37).

A contemplative, then, is called to protect inner solitude in every part of his life as a necessary precondition for contemplation. However, this is difficult in today's world because it goes against the grain of our fixation on electronic media and our compulsion to fill up the quiet spaces in our lives with activity. Noise follows us everywhere—into gas stations, libraries, coffee shops, and even our homes. The ubiquitous ring of a cell phone has become our mantra.

John's message is clear, however: We have little hope for union with God when there is no quiet in our lives. We need to cultivate an interior secret space, away from the daily commotion, so that we can hear the voice of love constantly addressing us. To be sure, solitude, for John, is not a matter of escaping our circumstances, but we need time alone to allow ourselves to know and nurture the breath of love. Inner solitude eventually becomes an ongoing sense of being anchored, even in the middle of distraction.

There is no better summary of the grace of solitude than John's *Spiritual Canticle*, in which he speaks of seeing the face of God in all nature and experiencing the "supper that refreshes."

My Beloved, the mountains,
and lonely wooded valleys,
strange islands,
and resounding rivers,
the whistling of love-stirring breezes,

the tranquil night
at the time of the rising dawn,
silent music,
sounding solitude,
the supper that refreshes, and deepens love.
(stanzas 14, 15)

Reading these lines returns me to a cottage in Canada that sat next to a quiet and still bay. During a sabbatical there, I was intent on creating a daily ritual that would strengthen solitude. One practice centered me more than the rest. Each morning, weather permitting, I woke up early and paddled a canoe into the hushed bay and waited in a soupy, gray mist for the first light of dawn to appear. At rest, sinking fully into the moment, I witnessed the first shafts of sunlight filtering through the mist, casting aside large smoky curtains. The water around me came alive, and the jagged outline of islands and trees arose from the mist. Reveling in the secret rhythm of this silence and solitude, I closed my eyes and waited. Throughout the day, I found myself returning to this awakening dawn to refresh my spirit.

Practicing Love

It should be noted that until the soul reaches this state of union of love, she should practice love in both the active and contemplative life. (Canticle 29.2)

It would be easy to assume that the call to solitude and contemplative prayer removes us from the world and that John was interested in addressing only hermits and monks who had separated themselves from the social involvement and the social issues we all face. In fact, he espoused a solitude that anchors us, whether we are religious or laypeople, even in the chaos of our daily schedules. According to John, contemplative solitude should give us the strength to practice love.

John's own life is a fundamental example of integration between the inner dimension of contemplation and the outer dimension of day-to-day responsibilities. He traveled extensively, spending a great deal of time on the road, on foot, overseeing priories and convents under his care. He was admired for his business acumen and ability to make wise, practical decisions. He enjoyed manual labor and would pitch in whenever he saw others working, whether it was sweeping a kitchen floor or laying brick. In towns that surrounded Carmelite priories and convents, he became a spiritual guide to people from every walk of life, from laborer to university professor.

Once, while visiting a convent, John saw a shoeless nun sweeping the floor. When he found out that she had no footwear, he solicited funds and gave them to her.[27] Perhaps this spontaneous compassion was learned from his mother, who cared for people who were needier than she was. Or perhaps the ground-work for service was laid when, as a young man, he worked in hospitals nursing those afflicted with the plague and venereal disease. It is certain, though, that it is difficult to read his life story without seeing how growth in contemplation engendered in him an extraordinary life of service to those in need.

We learn from John that contemplation cultivates a spiritual core, allowing us to transcend cultural values in such a way that we discover a deeper, more compassionate union with others in Christ. Because it gives us a sense of connecting with others on a deeper level, namely, the Mystical Body of Christ, contemplation intensifies the depth of our involvement.

In addition, a contemplative who demonstrates selfless giving takes a prophetic stance within the community. She exposes the illusion of a group of people bound together superficially by its diversions. Mesmerized by a constant stream of media, we can become so wrapped up in cultural interests that we fall asleep, lulled into a state of apathy. We lose any sense of the inherent solitude that we share with others, and as a result, we find it difficult to reach out in compassion and service.

John believed that our journey through the dark night wakes us up and teaches us a poverty of spirit that enables us to extend compassion. For example, in the beginning, the redirection of our desires toward God as our ultimate concern nurtures humility, an awareness of our true condition as a human being before God. Humility will not let us forget that we are not separate but one. In John's words, "From this humility stems love of neighbor, for they esteem them and do not judge them" (*Dark Night* I.12.8).

As the darkness moves from dusk to midnight, it produces a deep peace of soul that keeps us rooted even in the turmoil of constant change and activity. It also frees us to enjoy all things, physical and spiritual, as they were meant to be enjoyed: as gifts (*Dark Night* II.9.1). Furthermore, the rich inner growth in this darkness helps us focus on what is important in our daily lives, which is crucial in a consumer culture that links pursuit of desire to happiness and human identity to a commodity.

In the end, John believes that at the initial stage of our journey, the "Martha aspect" of the spiritual life is important, but he defends the "way of Mary"—the contemplative who has reached union with God—as primary. He writes that once a soul has arrived at the state of union of love, it "should not become involved in other works and exterior exercises that might be of the slightest hindrance to the attentiveness of the love toward God" (*Canticle* 29.2). His point is that a person fully engaged in contemplation has the power to do more for those in need than anyone dedicated to works of mercy.

The Garden of Love

One does not reach this garden of full transformation, which is the joy, delight, and glory of spiritual marriage, without first passing through the spiritual betrothal and the loyal and mutual love of betrothed persons. (Canticle 22.4)

At the close of his life, John revealed once again that love was the only reason for life and the entire motivation for his journey to God. Here is a biographer's account of John's last moments on earth:

> On Friday, December 13, 1591, Fray Juan knew instinctively that his death was close at hand. He asked to see the prior and begged forgiveness for all the difficulties he had caused him and the monks. The prior made excuses for not being able to offer him more because of the poverty of the house. The day was silent and cold. Occasionally, Fray Juan would ask what time it was. He seemed obsessed with the time. He would then close his eyes. At times the brothers thought he had died, but no, he was only being quiet. When he opened his eyes he would look at the crucifix at his bedside, kiss it and go back into silence. . . .
>
> . . . A few minutes later when the prior began saying the prayers for the dying, Fray Juan asked him to read instead some of the passages from the Song of Songs. As they were read, he kept repeating: "What marvelous pearls . . . "[28]

One of John's images for contemplative union with God is the garden found in the Songs of Songs. In this sacred poem, the garden landscape becomes the environment for the encounter between us, all of humanity, and God—lover and Beloved. In John's poetic response to the Song of Songs, *The Spiritual Canticle*, God breathes in the flowering garden of the soul, and all the buds open and riches pour out. The soul is overwhelmed by the beauty of the gifts, "and she rests in delight" (stanza 22). All relationships are included in this landscape: people, nature, and the divine. However, these relationships are no longer seen from our limited perspective but through a contemplative one, namely, through the eyes of God.

It is important to realize that according to John, contemplative union does not remove us from the earthiness of daily routine but grounds us even more deeply in it. The garden was important for him as a physical landscape. He could be found in the garden working the soil, planting, tending, and harvesting. He also shared his time with those who came to him for spiritual guidance and with his family.

To get a feel for the full potential of the garden symbol, imagine that you are entering a vegetable garden or exploring a meandering trail in a wooded garden. You walk through a gate and begin to follow a path. Your senses take in the scent of dank earth, the colors of fruit hanging from plants and trees, and the various textures of the vegetation. You listen to the sounds of birds and the rustle of a breeze through branches. Once you have settled into your personal garden, consider the Book of Genesis and how the garden represented what God meant creation to be. We once enjoyed walking with God in the garden, and then the plan collapsed through human weakness. But we walk a garden path once again because the dying and rising of Jesus has redeemed us. John guides us to a discovery of the fullness of this redemption through a dark night. In the dark night, our vision of the truth, our union with God, is restored.

As we have seen, through the gift of contemplation, God darkens and liberates us, pervades our entire being, healing all imperfection and disorder, and draws us toward union. We are meant for union, John reminds us, and every person's love relationship with God reaches fulfillment only in divine union. The highest state of union for John is spiritual marriage, which is a total transformation into the Beloved. It is a surrender of the entire self to the other in love. As a result, according to John, the soul becomes divine—it becomes God through participation (2 Peter 1:4). Though this is the highest state attainable in this life, John recognizes that even if we have not reached these heights of contemplation, we do enjoy a brief taste of union during graced moments of contemplative prayer.

This is an astounding revelation: My personal relationship with God is meant to reach completion in spiritual union and, in doing so, shares the life of the Trinity. Our entire lives are meant for one thing only: to share divine life. Yet how easy it is to be swayed by other things that present themselves as being more important! However, the seeker who willingly sacrifices for the sake of love becomes more and more restless and, forgetting herself, concentrates on her burning desire for God. Nothing deters the longings of love as each one of us swiftly and boldly moves toward union.

From the beginning, the journey has been one of prayer and love. *The Spiritual Canticle* provides an overview and shows us the importance of our longing for God. *The Ascent of Mount Carmel* prepares us for the journey by giving us the gift of freedom to find the Beloved. *The Dark Night* releases the love that is the Spirit's gift within us. John insists at every turn that this journey makes us like God and opens our hearts to others and to the cosmos.

Who can put into language the experience of divine love? John invites us into the mystery of God, into that "secret and peaceful and loving inflow of God" (*Dark Night* I.10.6) that we call contemplation. As contemplation grows and flame turns to fire, our longing for the divine increases. We desire God with an urgency that John recognizes as our call: "This enkindling of love occurs in the spirit. Through it the soul in the midst of these dark conflicts feels vividly and keenly that it is being wounded by a strong divine love, and it has a certain feeling and foretaste of God" (*Dark Night* II.11.1). The dark night does not last forever. A new energy is released in our depths and rises up; our eyes begin to see the dawn as we have never seen it before.

Suggestions for Reflection

1. When have you heard God whispering in the silence, drawing you into the garden of your own soul? When have you heard the urge to remain quiet with Elijah on the mountain (1 Kings 19:9-13)? How are you responding?

2. How has your faith deepened in the dark times you have experienced? Do you trust the darkness as the inflow of love that holds the promise of light?

3. Imagine an inner garden. In the morning, when you are in the garden, it refreshes the soul and gives it an awareness of the possibilities of new life. Where are these possibilities arising in your life?

   In the night the silence of the garden becomes a nourishing environment drawing the soul home to rest. When have you found yourself drawn to rest deeply in God's love?

Take a moment and let this image of the garden, morning and evening, bring you back into the presence of Love. If this image is attractive to you, return to it whenever you find your mind wandering.

Suggested Reading

Brennan, Gerald. *St. John of the Cross: His Life and Poetry*. London: Cambridge University Press, 1973.

Burrows, Ruth. *Ascent to Love: The Spiritual Teaching of St. John of the Cross*. Denville, NJ: Dimension Books, 1987.

Collings, Ross. *John of the Cross. Way of Christian Mystics,* 10. Collegeville, MN: Liturgical Press, Michael Glazier, 1990.

Dombrowski, Daniel A. *St. John of the Cross: An Appreciation*. Albany, NY: State University Press, 1992.

Doohan, Leonard. *The Contemporary Challenge of John of the Cross: An Introduction to His Life and Teaching*. Washington, DC: ICS Publications, 1995.

Matthew, Iaian. *The Impact of God: Soundings from St. John of the Cross*. London: Hodder & Stoughton, 1995.

May, Gerald G. *The Dark Night of the Soul*. New York: HarperCollins Publishers, Inc., 2004.

Merton, Thomas. *The Ascent to Truth*. New York: Harcourt Brace, 1951.

Muto, Susan. *John of the Cross for Today: The Dark Night*. Notre Dame, IN: Ave Maria Press, 1991.

Payne, Steven, and others. *John of the Cross: Conferences and Essays*. Carmelite Studies 6. Washington, DC: ICS Publications, 1992.

Tavard, George. *Poetry and Contemplation in St. John of the Cross*. Athens, OH: Ohio University Press, 1988.

Welch, John. *When Gods Die: An Introduction to John of the Cross*. Mahwah, NJ: Paulist Press, 1990.

Wojtyla, Karol. *Faith According to St. John of the Cross*. San Francisco: Ignatius Press, 1981.

ENDNOTES

1. *God Speaks in the Night: The Life, Times, and Teachings of St. John of the Cross*, trans. Kieran Kavanaugh, OCD (Washington, DC: ICS Publications, 1991), 153.

2. Thomas Merton, *Disputed Questions* (New York: Farrar, Straus and Cudahy, 1960), 214–215.

3. Richard Hardy, *Search for Nothing: The Life of John of the Cross* (New York: Crossroad, 1989), 111.

4. Leonard Doohan, *The Contemporary Challenge of John of the Cross: An Introduction to His Life and Teaching* (Washington, DC: ICS Publications, 1995), 113.

5. William Shannon, *Silence on Fire: Prayer of Awareness* (New York: Crossroad, 2000), 47.

6. Henri Nouwen, *The Return of the Prodigal Son* (New York: Image Books, 1992), 17.

7. John Welch, O Carm, *An Introduction to John of the Cross: When Gods Die* (New York: Paulist Press, 1990), 28–29.

8. Ed. Robert Ellsberg, *Dorothy Day: Selected Writings* (New York: Orbis Books, 1993), 9.

9. Leo Tolstoy, *The Death of Ivan Ilyich* (New York: Bantam Books, 1981), 126.

10. Holly Bridges Eliot, *Beholding God in Many Faces* (Winona, MN: St. Mary's Press, 1993), 74, 77.

11. Thomas Merton, *Seven Storey Mountain* (New York: Harcourt Brace Jovanovich, 1948), 3.

12. Bernard Bagley, *Talks on the Song of Songs* (Brewster, MA: Paraclete Press, 2002), 17.

13. *The Collected Works of St. John of the Cross,* rev. ed., trans. Kieran Kavanaugh, OCD, and Otilio Rodriguez, OCD (Washington, DC: ICS Publications), 37.

14. Wilfred McGreal, O Carm, *At the Fountain of Elijah: The Carmelite Tradition* (New York: Orbis Books, 1999), 13.

15. *The Collected Poems of Thomas Merton* (New York: New Directions, 1980), 104–105.

16. Crisogono de Jesus, *The Life of St. John of the Cross* (New York: Harper & Brothers, 1958), 134.

17. *The Practice of the Presence of God*, trans. John J. Delaney (New York: Image Books, 1977), 68, 70.

18. Henri Nouwen, *Sabbatical Journey* (New York: Crossroad, 1998), 5–6.

19. Crisogono de Jesus, *The Life of St. John of the Cross,* 207–208.

20. Richard Hardy, *Search for Nothing,* 66, 70.

21. Belden Lane, *The Solace of Fierce Landscapes* (New York: Oxford University Press, 2007), 19.

22. Gerald G. May, *The Dark Night of the Soul* (San Francisco: HarperCollins Publishers, 2004), 95.

23. Belden Lane, *The Solace of Fierce Landscapes,* 180.

24. Thomas Keating, *The Human Condition* (New York: Paulist Press, 1999), 40.

25. Nikos Kazantzakis, *Report to Greco* (New York: Bantam Books, 1966), 286.

26. Crisogono de Jesus, *The Life of St. John of the Cross*, 288.

27. Crisogono de Jesus, *The Life of St. John of the Cross*, 75–76.

28. Richard Hardy, *Search for Nothing*, 110–111.

the WORD among us®
The Spirit of Catholic Living

This book was published by The Word Among Us. For thirty years, The Word Among Us has been answering the call of the Second Vatican Council to help Catholic laypeople encounter Christ in the Scriptures—a call reiterated by Pope Benedict XVI and a Synod of Bishops.

The name of our company comes from the prologue to the Gospel of John and reflects the vision and purpose of all of our publications: to be an instrument of the Spirit, whose desire is to manifest Jesus' presence in and to the children of God. In this way we hope to contribute to the Church's ongoing mission of proclaiming the gospel to the world and growing ever more deeply in our love for the Lord.

Our monthly devotional magazine, *The Word Among Us*, features meditations on the daily and Sunday Mass readings, and currently reaches more than one million Catholics in North America each year and another 500,000 Catholics in 100 countries. Our press division has published nearly 200 books and Bible studies over the past 12 years.

To learn more about who we are and what we publish, log on to our Web site at **www.wau.org**. There you will find a variety of Catholic resources that will help you grow in your faith.

Embrace His Word, Listen to God . . .

www.wau.org